CREATIVE RECORDING

Soundproofing, Acoustics and Monitoring

Published by Music Maker books

Alexander House, Forehill, Ely

Cambridgeshire, England.

© Paul White 1991

ISBN 1 870951 09 3

Editor:	Paul White
Illustrations:	Paul White
Layout and Setting:	Paul White & Music Maker Books
Cover Illustration:	Stuart Catterson
Printing:	Watkiss Studios Limited, Biggleswade

First published in Great Britain 1991
Second printing February 1993

DEDICATIONS

This book is dedicated to my daughter Emma who has changed my attitude towards soundproofing from casual interest to life or death necessity!

Thanks to Debbie Poyser for her (once again unpaid) proof reading.

CREATIVE RECORDING

Soundproofing, Acoustics and Monitoring

Paul White

CONTENTS

INTRODUCTION

**CONCEPTS OF
SOUNDPROOFING**

Sound Energy	1
Low Frequencies	2
Double Walls	2
Problem Areas	2
Floors	3
Overview	4
Premises	4
Technical Notes	5

PRACTICAL APPROACHES

Uprating	7
Walls	7
Studding Wall	8
Panelling	8
Wall Uprating	9
Sealing	10
Improvisation	11

DOORS AND WINDOWS

Doors	13
Double Doors	15
Windows	16
Triple Glazing	17
Patio Doors	18
Summary	19

FLOORS AND CEILINGS

Floors	21
Floating Floor	21
Lightweight Floors	22
Floating Raft	24
Ceilings	24
Suspended Ceilings	25

FLOATING ROOMS

Doors	27
Monitor Isolation	29
Windows	30
Voids	31

ACOUSTIC TREATMENTS

Listening Environment	34
Room parameters	34
Modes	35
Optimum Dimensions	35
Bolt's Graph	37
Adaptation	38
Absorbers	38
Resonant Traps	39
Panel Absorber	39
Damping	40
Helmholz Traps	41

Mid and High Absorbers 43
Movable Screens 43

DESIGN CRITERIA
T60 46
Pragmatism 46
Sabine 47
Absorption Units 47
Distribution 48
Doing the Sums 49
Flutter Echo 49
Useful Absorption Coefficients 50

CONTROL ROOM DESIGN
Dimensions 53
Target Reverb Time 55
Anechoic Rooms 55
Philosophy 56
Live or Dead 56
Haas Effect 57
LEDE 57
Diffusion 58
LEDE Limitations 59
Trapping 60
Tuned Traps 61

THE STUDIO
Variable Acoustics 63

MONITORS
The Ideal Monitor 67
Crossovers 68
Multi-Way 69
Driver types 70
Woofers 70
Mid Range 71
Tweeters 71

Dual Concentric 71
Phase 72
Off-Axis Response 73
Dips and Bumps 74

MONITOR SYSTEMS
Amplifier Ratings 75
Peaks 76
Protection 76
Wiring 77

MONITORS AND ROOMS
Geometry 80
Stands 80
Corners 81
Soffit Mounting 83
Near-Field Monitoring 83
Monitor Equalisation 84

BUDGET ROOMS
Monitors 85
Mixer 86
Impromptu Acoustics 86
Larger Home Studios 86
Total Treatment 87
What System 88
LEDE 89

SUMMARY
Source 91
DI'ing 91
Optimum Acoustics 92
Monitor Requirements 92
Realistic Aims 93
Rational Approach 93
Air Conditioning 94
Materials 95

INTRODUCTION

Many people still confuse soundproofing with acoustic treatment. Soundproofing deals with keeping unwanted sound from getting in or out of a room while acoustic treatment deals more with the acoustic quality of the room from a listener's point of view.

In the typical home studio, soundproofing often needs to be a lot higher on the priority list than acoustic treatment, largely due to the need to coexist in a peaceable manner with the rest of the neighbourhood. Obviously this not only involves preventing sound escaping but also unwanted sound from getting in.

Acoustic treatment, on the other hand, generally relates to the way in which sound is reflected or absorbed within a room to create a suitable listening environment and the requirements will vary depending on whether the room is to be used as a voice-over studio, a music studio or a live music venue.

The purpose of this book is to explore the basic rules of acoustics as applied first to soundproofing, then to creating a good listening environment. Practical applications are described throughout, most of which are within the scope of a competent DIY enthusiast. Most of the materials used can be obtained from any good builders' merchant, but there are some specialised materials and a source of supply (UK only) is included in the notes at the end of this book. Please forgive the occasional mixture of imperial and SI units of measurement - I've used the units most often applied to the materials in question.

There's also a section on monitor systems which will help you choose the right system for your room as well as advising on their installation and suitable amplification.

CONCEPTS OF SOUNDPROOFING

At the outset, it is important to differentiate between sound-proofing or sound isolation, and acoustic treatment. Sound isolation is concerned only with preventing unwanted sound from either entering or leaving the building while acoustic treatment deals with creating a suitable listening environment for recording or mixing.

There exists a popular myth that sticking egg boxes to the inside walls of a room will prevent sound from escaping, but unfortunately, life isn't that simple. Fixing cardboard egg cartons to the walls may well shorten the top end reverberation time of a room to some degree, but it will do virtually nothing to stop sound from escaping or unwanted noise from entering.

SOUND ENERGY

Before trying to contain or keep out sound, we need to know a little about its nature. Sound is a form of energy which propagates by mechanical vibration through gases, liquids and solids. The law of conservation of energy states that energy cannot simply be told to go away - it must be converted to another form or remain in its present one. The reason sound doesn't continue forever is because its energy is absorbed by the surfaces that it encounters and the air that it passes through, changing it to heat in the process. Even very loud sounds contain relatively little energy so the amount of heat created by sound dissipation in a typical studio is, to all intents and purposes, negligible.

In soundproofing, our main problem is to try to persuade as much sound as possible to convert itself to heat before it either gets in through the walls of our studio or out into the neighbour's house. What keeps sound in also keeps it out, and the simplest form of sound attenuator is a nice solid wall which will both reflect and absorb some of the sound. There's a useful physical law that's worth remembering: if you double the mass of the wall, you'll roughly halve the amount of sound transmitted. To put it another way, we can attenuate the sound by, at best, 6dB each time we double the mass of a wall. In practice, resonances reduce this figure to nearer 5dB.

LOW FREQUENCIES

Another very important point is that soundproofing becomes less effective the lower the frequency. Every time you drop the sound by an octave, the isolation provided by the wall is halved. That makes it a relatively simple matter to keep out treble and mid-range frequencies, but the deeper the bass, the bigger the problem. Because attenuation is frequency-dependent, the effectiveness of a sound absorbing partition is often measured in dBs for a range of frequencies averaged over the range 100Hz to just over 3kHz, and this figure is given the grand title of the Sound Reduction Index. A typical figure might be in the order of 45dB for a single brick wall and 50dB for a solid double-brick thickness wall. In practical terms, this means that if your music is loud, the level at the other side of the wall, though much reduced, will still be heard, particularly at the bass end. If you are directly adjoining a neighbour, this will probably still be unacceptably loud.

DOUBLE WALLS

It doesn't take a great mental leap to consider the possibility of erecting a double wall with an air gap in between and this is indeed a great improvement. You might, not unreasonably, think that 45dB for one wall added to 45dB for the next would give a 90dB figure, which would be a terrific. However, it's not quite as effective as you might think unless the walls are separated by several feet. That's clearly not so practical!

At smaller distances, the air loading between the walls does some strange and often complicated things which inevitably reduce the sound isolation, and often the easiest way to find out what the actual SRI is going to be, is to build the thing and measure it. However, it's a universal truth that separate layers separated by air gaps or absorbing material do work better than one thick wall.

PROBLEM AREAS

Before looking at practical sound isolation techniques, we should review the main problem areas in a typical home studio: doors and windows. Despite what the glossy ads may imply, even double glazed windows offer no more than a very limited amount of sound isolation and a significant amount of sound will still pass through. Worthwhile DIY improvements might take the form of extra glazing with a large air gap and heavy glass, or you could opt to invoke the mass law and fill the window space with sandbags, concrete blocks or purpose-built shutters. Heavy curtains also help but are not a solution in themselves. I'll be looking at some practical solutions later on in the book.

It's also surprising just how much sound gets through and around a door. Because they don't generally fit as tightly as windows, and because of the lightness of modern interior doors, significant improvements can be made by attending to this area. Solutions include fitting good door seals, adding mass to the door, building multi-layer doors and fitting double doors. If you can afford it, a solid wooden fire door in a well fitting frame is a good investment.

FLOORS

Concrete floors don't represent an overwhelming problem unless you want to achieve a very high level of sound insulation, but wooden floors certainly do. Even if you build a proper floating false floor, it's very unlikely that you will be able to use a real drum kit without causing some disturbance to those below unless you go to great expense. If it's your own house, then it may be effective enough to make life tolerable for the rest of the household if they're of an understanding nature, but if you have a flat full of non-musicians below you, then you may have to forget real drums.

Ceilings are very expensive to soundproof effectively, and short of suspending tons of concrete slabs, woodwool or sandbags over your head, the most effective compromise may be to buy a couple of layers of thick underfelt for the people upstairs and play a little quieter. However, depending on how much sound isolation you need to achieve, there are practical DIY solutions which will be covered in the appropriate chapters.

Professional studio designers tackle the problem by building a separate inner room which is isolated from the outer walls, floors and ceilings of the main building, but apart from the obvious cost factor, most home studios simply don't have the available space. However, if you have the space and are keen on DIY, the constructional techniques involved are covered later and the cost may be a lot lower than you think. The other advantage of this 'room within a room' system is that it behaves relatively predictably when it comes to adding internal acoustic treatment.

OVERVIEW

Despite the fact that it appears all of nature's cards are stacked against ever achieving decent sound isolation, there are various degrees of sound insulation that can be applied, and in terms of expense, time and effectiveness, the law of diminishing returns applies as it does in most things. By applying a little common sense and using the principles outlined in this book, you should be able to make a substantial improvement to the sound insulation of your studio and also improve its performance as a listening room.

The underlying concepts are, that to isolate sound, you need structural mass, air-tight seals and some method of isolating against structure-borne sound. This latter consideration is very important because sound travels very efficiently through solid structures such as wooden joists or steel girders. There's no point in getting everything else right if your soundproofing is short-circuited by an unfortunate piece of structure.

Soundproof generally means airtight and that doesn't bode well for ventilation. A proper studio air conditioner with silencer baffles and anti-vibration mountings costs more than most complete home studios, so obviously some compromise must be sought.

PREMISES

If you are choosing new premises in which to set up a studio, you can save yourself a considerable amount of time and expense by first taking into account the existing structure of the building, its location and any industrial activities taking place in or near it. Ideally, you should choose a ground floor premises in a solidly-built brick or concrete building because you'll almost certainly have the benefits of a solid floor, there'll be nobody underneath you to annoy, and a ground floor setup is easier for access. You'll also have to consider the rooms above the studio if you don't actually own them, especially if they are part of a business premises that might suddenly change its use from flower arranging to heavy sheet metal work or, worse still, to a night club.

You should also listen out for low frequency rumble from traffic or trains, and if this is in evidence, you'll need a proper floating floor to reduce it to acceptable levels.

If you must accept an upstairs premises, then find out what is happening above, below and to either side of you, and whether the rooms are occupied at night. Additionally, if you are planning to do any serious acoustic treatment or build a full room-within-a-room studio, then you must allow space for the acoustic treatment, not only with regard to the walls but also the available ceiling height. If you are going to build even a simple inner shell, you should ideally have a couple of feet more headroom than you'll ultimately need, though at a pinch, you can just about get away with a little less.

Though the new floor may only take up four inches or so, the inner ceiling needs to be spaced as far as possible from the original ceiling to achieve reasonable low frequency isolation. The ceiling may also have to be deep enough to accommodate bass trapping, depending on the type of acoustic design approach you take and whether there is other available space, such as deep wall alcoves, that can be utilised for this purpose.

TECHNICAL NOTES

For the mathematically inclined, there's a simple formula that enables you to work out the Sound Reduction Index or SRI of a solid wall based on the mass per square metre of the wall material. Note that the answer depends on the frequency of the sound we are trying to attenuate.

$$R=20 \log(fm)-47dB$$

f is the frequency of the incident sound

m is the mass of the wall measured in kg/m2

R is the Sound Reduction Index we are trying to calculate

A few sample calculations can reveal some interesting facts concerning popular building materials, though non-solid materials behave differently from solid ones and real-life measurement is often the only sure-fire way of checking how they will actually perform. For example, a light panelled door such as is used in modern house construction has an average SRI of around only 15dB and at low frequencies, it will be significantly worse than that.

On the other hand, a double brick thickness cavity wall, plastered on the inside, can have an average SRI in excess of 50dB.

PRACTICAL APPROACHES

UPRATING

If you are building a commercial studio or if you make a living from your recorded music, then you may be able to afford the cost and have the space to build a proper room-within-a-room studio. Certainly if you live in a residential area and want to be able to record live music at all hours of the day and night, there is unlikely to be any other satisfactory solution. However, most private and home studios do not operate 24 hours a day so it may be possible to time particularly noisy activities such as the recording of drums so as not to cause undue inconvenience to the neighbours by waiting until they go out. In this case, uprating the existing structure may be adequate.

Firstly, you'll need to check out the walls, floors, ceilings, windows and doors to see what sound isolation problems currently exist. Once the weak spots have been identified, you should address the most problematic areas first. Like the proverbial chain, sound isolation is only as effective as its weakest link!

WALLS

Brick or stone walls are not usually the greatest problem when it comes to home studio soundproofing, but lighter walls present difficulties, especially if one or more walls is a light studding partition. The same applies if you want to build a new sound-isolating internal wall or if a next door neighbour is only one layer of breeze block away from your drum booth. But even if your walls are all solid brick, a further improvement can be made using the techniques described.

In the event that a new solid wall needs to be constructed, whether internal or external, the ideal choice is a cavity construction (with few or no ties bridging the cavity) consisting of brick or concrete blocks if at all possible; breeze blocks are too light and consequently offer poor low frequency attenuation. If a solid internal wall is impractical, then a well constructed studding wall can be very effective.

STUDDING WALL

Because a simple studding wall doesn't usually have the necessary mass to be a good absorber, we have to resort to a few tricks to improve the situation. Two thin walls are more effective than one thicker one so a double skinned structure is preferable if you have the space to accommodate it. The first step is to construct a frame from 2" x 4" studding - but you have to be careful how you fix this in place. Remember that sound travels quite happily within solids, so it's essential to ensure that the frame doesn't make a good acoustic contact with the floor, the walls or the ceiling. Sadly, gravity is against us on this one so some degree of acoustic coupling is inevitable.

The best compromise is to insert 1/4" thick (or thicker) neoprene sheeting (a synthetic, hardish, rubber-like material) between the frame and the floor to support it and to use a similar approach where the wall touches other walls and the ceiling. If you can't find a local supplier of neoprene, check Yellow Pages for rubber, foam and plastics suppliers; they should be able to point you in the right direction. You can also use a thick rubber car floor mat chopped into strips or even strips of insulation board at a pinch.

Some screws will have to pass through the neoprene to hold the studding wall in place, and of course these will transmit some sound, but there's always a necessary degree of compromise. Even so, screws normally go into Rawlplugs in the wall and these decouple a little of the sound energy.

PANELLING

The frame is then panelled over on both sides with not one but two layers of plasterboard, preferably the 12mm thick type. Having two layers increases the mass, and hence the sound isolation of the structure, and the layers damp each other reducing the risk of resonances. Ensure that the joins in the plasterboard are staggered and ideally, have the surface skimmed with plaster on completion.

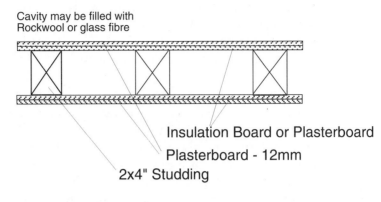

Cavity may be filled with
Rockwool or glass fibre

Insulation Board or Plasterboard

Plasterboard - 12mm

2x4" Studding

Skim surface with plaster after
completion

Figure 2.1: Construction of a Studding Wall

Figure 2.1 shows how such a studding wall might be constructed. The partition can be made even more effective by building two separate frameworks with the studs staggered to fit between each other. This reduces the mechanical coupling between the two sides of the wall and only requires a couple of inches or so extra space. Figure 2.2 illustrates this alternative.

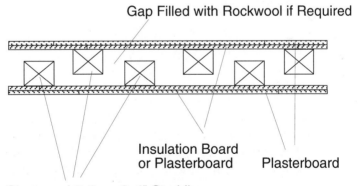

Gap Filled with Rockwool if Required

Insulation Board
or Plasterboard   Plasterboard

Staggered 2x2 or 2x4" Studding

Figure 2.2: Staggered Stud Partition

WALL UPRATING

If you're lining an existing wall, then the construction is similar except you only need to cover one side of the frame and you should leave a small gap between the frame and the existing wall. The cavities within the frame between the existing wall and the new skin can be filled with Rockwool or glass fibre and then the plasterboard skin nailed in place.

Rockwool works rather better than fibreglass, even though it costs slightly more, and your local builder's merchant should be able to get it for you by the roll. Alternatively, 2" Rockwool slab is slighly more effective and easier to handle, though it does cost more.

Once again, greater mass is applied by using two (or more) layers of plasterboard or by layering plasterboard, chipboard and fibre insulation board to form a sound-deadening sandwich. Layering different materials is a good idea as it provides a deliberate acoustic mismatch causing vibrations to reflect back and forth within the structure increasing the likelihood of absorption. Figure 2.3 shows this method of uprating.

Existing Wall

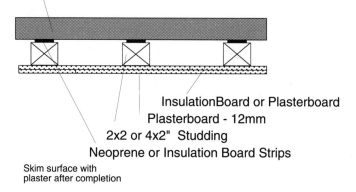

InsulationBoard or Plasterboard
Plasterboard - 12mm
2x2 or 4x2" Studding
Neoprene or Insulation Board Strips

Skim surface with
plaster after completion

Figure 2.3: Uprated Wall

SEALING

Studding partitions will be more efficient if the plasterboard surface doesn't touch the floor, ceiling or the existing walls. Leave a small gap which can be filled with a silicon rubber sealant or mastic. It's important that the joint is quite airtight. If you are using a multi-layer construction method, it's best to seal each layer with mastic before fixing the next layer. Even when all these precautions have been taken, the attenuation at low frequencies will be less than that offered by a solid brick wall, but substantial nonetheless.

The more layers you can use, the better the sound isolation will be, which is why professionally constructed studio walls sometimes have panels four inches or more in thickness. If you intend to go this far, make sure that the floor of your room will take the weight, and if you aren't sure, seek the advice of a reputable builder.

IMPROVISATION

No two rooms are quite the same, and an understanding of the basic principles will help you to apply some simple soundproofing techniques to your particular situation. Firstly, the greater the mass, the more work the sound has to do to move it, so a large mass is definitely good news for attenuation. Sound also travels well through solids, so anything you can do to isolate one solid section from the next, such as incorporating rubber, air gaps or other absorbent materials will help.

Acoustically absorbent material such as glass fibre or Rockwool can help when placed between partitions, and of course, don't forget to make sure that everything is absolutely airtight. But don't be tempted to put the Rockwool or glass fibre in plastic bags for convenience's sake or it won't do its job - air needs to be able to move in and out of the fibrous structure for absorption to occur. Open weave cloth bags are OK and help prevent the dust these materials produce.

Glass fibre and Rockwool are irritants, so wear gloves and a face mask whilst doing the job.

If you do need to build an internal wall, then read the section on acoustic treatment before you make a start. The ratio of the height, width and length of the room you build affect how they sound and it also matters whether walls are parallel or not. Professional designs tend to avoid parallel walls because they can cause flutter echoes and comb filtering effects, so are to be avoided if at all possible. Designers take this into account and calculate the optimum angles for all the walls, but at home, you're generally stuck with what you've got so you just have to make the best of it.

DOORS AND WINDOWS

So far, we've established that steps taken to prevent sound from leaving the studio also prevent it entering. But whether problems arise from noisy neighbours or loud lorries, the doors and windows are usually the first candidates for treatment. The reasons behind this are two-fold:

Firstly, doors and windows, unless they are modern double glazed units, are likely to be less than a perfect fit and it only takes a tiny gap to allow the sound to pour through. Checking the door for sound leakage is easy enough; leave a light on in the studio at night and then examine the edges of the frame for chinks of light. Windows you can inspect by feeling for draughts in windy weather.

Secondly, even blocking up all these gaps is not a complete solution - the problem being that the mass of doors and windows tends to be significantly less than that of the surrounding walls. We'll look at doors first because, though it may be possible to build a studio without windows, one without doors is not really a practical proposition.

DOORS

In a modern building, internal doors are often made from veneered ply panels with little between them except corrugated cardboard, and even in the majority of older houses, the doors are likely to be made up of panels which are far too light to attenuate sound adequately. The only real solution is to replace the door with something heavier or add a heavy layer to the existing door. Two layers of 3/4" ply or chipboard are reasonably cost effective. In extreme cases, people have been known to fill a hollow door with sand or even concrete to add the necessary mass, but this inevitably means replacing the door frame with something much stronger and using heavy duty hinges.

If you intend to build your own doors from two layers of thick ply or chipboard, leave a gap between the two layers of ply and use Rockwool or fibreglass to fill the remaining space. This will help to deaden any vibration of the panels and also absorb a proportion of the sound trying to radiate from one panel to the other. Because chipboard is not a structurally strong material, hard wood insets need to be used to take the hinges. Plywood is much stronger, and though more expensive, it makes the job a lot easier. Figure 3.1 should give you the general idea.

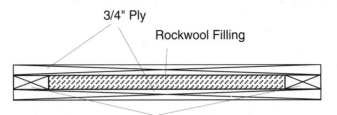

3/4" Ply

Rockwool Filling

Softwood

Figure 3.1: Constructing a Solid Door

The two panels are held about an inch apart with softwood batten. Alternatively, if planning a commercial studio, you could buy a heavy wood fire door. Once the door has been hung on fairly hefty hinges, make sure that the seal is airtight all the way round by fitting a proper sealing system.

The cheapest and most effective way to seal a door is to use a half-round gasket fitted to the door frame, (including the bottom), in conjunction with a pressure latch. These are mechanically simple latches that work by running up a tapered plastic wedge screwed to the door frame and so the door is forced against the seal as the handle is closed. The best seal material is made from a foam neoprene about one inch wide and the surface is covered with solid neoprene to make it more robust.

The easiest way to install such a system is to fit a plain door frame and then hang the door. Then, the door jambs are cut to size with mitred corners and the sealing strip glued to this with contact adhesive before the jambs are fitted in place. With the latch in its half closed position, the jambs should be tacked into place so that the seal just touches the door all the way round. This way, once the latch is fully closed, the seal will not be over-compressed and so won't tend to warp the door. Once you're sure the

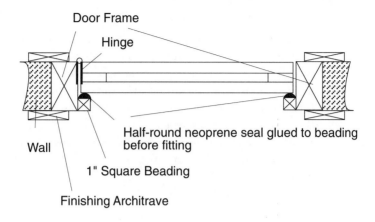

Door Frame

Hinge

Half-round neoprene seal glued to beading before fitting

Wall

1" Square Beading

Finishing Architrave

Figure 3.2: Door Gasket Details

door is fitting correctly, you can screw the jambs permanently into place. Figure 3.2 shows how this sealing system works.

Some studio designers even use the magnetic seals normally found on freezer or fridge doors. These have the advantage of good sealing properties, even when there is a slight gap between the door and frame, but they are expensive and suffer damage easily.

DOUBLE DOORS

Just as two walls separated by an air-gap will offer better sound isolation than one thick wall, two solid doors, fitted with seals will work appreciably better than one door on its own. Indeed, for any kind of loud music involving drums and amplified instruments, double doors are essential.

Where space is restricted, it is quite acceptable to use two outward opening doors on a single wall. This gives an air gap of around the thickness of the wall and doesn't take up any of your valuable space. Nevertheless, if you can arrange for a larger gap between the doors, the low frequency isolation will be better. If the gap is more than around three feet, you can safely use a simple spring closer on one of the doors rather than a pressure latch as the slight reduction in sealing efficiency will have only a small effect. This also makes life easier when carrying equipment through the doors.

It's advisable to use separate doorframes rather than one wide one, if at all possible, when building a double door. This is to prevent vibration travelling from the first door, along the frame and directly to the second door. To this end, frames are often isolated from the surrounding brickwork and from each other using Neoprene sheeting. This might be a little extreme for home use, but is worthwhile if building a studio from scratch or converting a garage. Gaps may be filled using expanding foam filler or mastic. Figure 3.3 shows a typical double door built into a single wall.

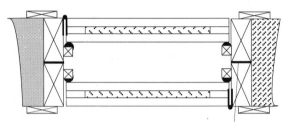

Compression handles must be used in order to get an effective seal

Two-part frame with mastic in the gap i

Figure 3.3: Double Door

WINDOWS

If the windows are of the old wooden sash type, then they really should be replaced by a modern double glazed unit unless you're prepared to lose all natural light by fitting a shutter. Should you choose the latter

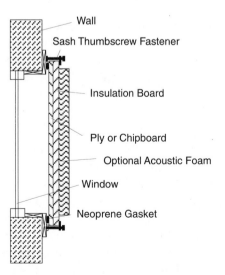

Figure 3.4: Simple Window Shutter

approach, use the same technique as for building the door, but clamp it in place with sash window thumbscrew fasteners rather than hinges, so that it can be removed quickly and easily. If, on the other hand, you intend to leave it closed for long periods, you could even run round the edge with a mastic gun to ensure a really airtight seal.

The inside face of the shutter may be covered with cork tiles, carpet or acoustic foam if you want to make it visually attractive or render it a little less reflective. The outside could benefit from being painted black with a dummy pair of curtains stapled in place. If you simply leave a bare board showing, the place will look like a strip club! Constructional details of a simple shutter are outlined in Figure 3.4.

If, on the other hand, light is important, and the basic window must be left as it is, secondary double glazing is a good approach, even if the existing window is already double glazed. One of the commercially fitted or DIY secondary glazing systems should suffice if the basic window is sound and well fitting, but use the heaviest grade of glass possible and contrive to leave the largest possible air gap between the original window and the secondary glazing.

A better alternative is to fit a completely new double-glazed window on the inside of your window opening, again with as large a gap as possible between it and the existing window.

If you can take out the existing windows and start from scratch, then I'd recommend aluminium or UPVC double glazed window units fitted to both the inside and the outside of the window opening giving you a total of four panes of glass in all. This approach is especially recommended if you use real drums and amplified guitars close to other residents.

TRIPLE GLAZING

A commercial studio installation typically uses heavy plate glass - usually three sheets separated by large gaps. Ideally the glass should be mounted so that the panes are not quite parallel, so as to prevent standing waves, and a Rockwool absorber might be used within the structure of the frame between the panes of glass to help mop up any sound energy that tries to pass through the air gap. The glass would also be mounted on Neoprene rather than directly into a wooden frame, to prevent structurally borne transmission. Figure 3.5 illustrates this form of mounting with a simple way of implementing a Rockwool absorber. For cosmetic purposes, the entrance to the Rockwool filled cavity can be covered using any suitable porous fabric or even pegboard.

Frame sections separated by mastic

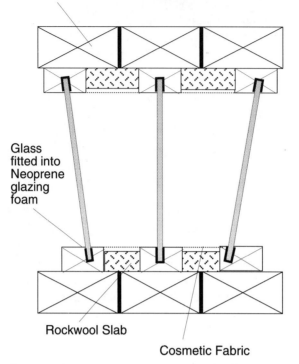

Glass
fitted into
Neoprene
glazing
foam

Rockwool Slab

Cosmetic Fabric

Figure 3.5: Triple Glazed Studio Window

Exactly the same philosophy applies to control room windows where a minimum of two and ideally three sheets of plate glass should be mounted on Neoprene in a non-parallel configuration and with as large an air gap as is practical. It is also more important than ever, in this application, to use different thicknesses of glass so that any resonances in the panes occur at different frequencies.

PATIO DOORS

There has been a trend in recent years to use patio door to divide the studio and the control room because they double as a viewing window and as a means of access. In order to achieve sufficient sound isolation to allow working with live rock music, two sets of double-glazed patio doors must be used with an air gap between them of at least two feet. Any less than this and the bass isolation will be seriously compromised. This large air gap also compensates for deficiencies in the door seals. The walls within the cavity formed by the two sets of door should be lined with Rockwool or acoustic foam to a depth of at least two inches. Figure 3.6 shows a typical installation.

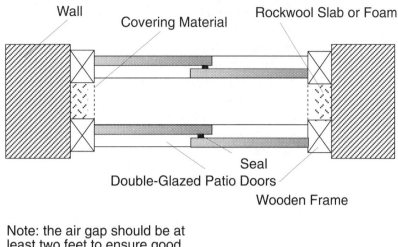

Wall

Covering Material

Rockwool Slab or Foam

Seal

Double-Glazed Patio Doors

Wooden Frame

Note: the air gap should be at
least two feet to ensure good
isolation

Figure 3.6: Double Patio Doors

SUMMARY

There are obviously several ways to achieve the same objective, and the
main thing is to keep in mind the basic rules, then make your own
decisions based on financial resources and requirements. Doors need to be
as heavy as possible, with an airtight fit, and a double door assembly is
always best, space permitting. Sound also travels quite happily through
solids so Neoprene sheet can be used to advantage to isolate structures
such as door frames from their surroundings.

Rockwool stuffed into air gaps will help to damp panels and also absorb a
little of the airborne sound trying to cross the gap. Aerosol polyurethane
foam is useful for filling small gaps and it also has strong adhesive
properties making it ideal for fixing frames without allowing the sound to
travel across into the structure.

Windows follow a similar philosophy, and because there is a limit to the
thickness, and hence mass, of window pane you can use, double or triple
glazing is invariably the best answer unless the windows can be blocked
up entirely. Again, they should be airtight, and for best results, the
individual panes should be isolated from their respective frames using
Neoprene or proprietary foam-rubber glass mounting strip.

Even when all these steps have been taken, the sound leakage through the doors and windows is still likely to be greater than that through the walls, especially at low frequencies where brute mass forms the only really effective barrier. Nevertheless, the difference can be dramatic and may make all the difference between a studio that is workable and one that isn't. As mentioned at the beginning of the article, the windows and doors of an existing building are by far the worst areas of sound leakage, so it's pointless doing anything else to the room until these problem areas have been tackled.

FLOORS AND CEILINGS

FLOORS

In home studio soundproofing, floors often represent serious problem areas, especially if the studio is in your bedroom and the rest of the household is below, trying to lead a quiet life. Due to the constraints of gravity, a lot of noise-producing equipment is likely to be located on the floor: amplifiers, drum kits, speakers and the like. Therefore structurally-borne sound needs to be tackled. Furthermore, the mass of a conventional wooden floor isn't going to be anywhere near as much as that of a brick or concrete wall, so low frequency sound generated within the room can pass through quite easily.

The cheapest compromise approach is to install a heavy felt underlay beneath the studio carpet and then isolate all the noise producing equipment from the floor. For instance, speakers can be wall-mounted or placed on shelves and guitar amps can be stood on blocks of foam rubber. Isolating your speakers from the shelves or wall brackets using chunks of Blu-Tak will also help to reduce structurally-borne sound. Drum kits, though, tend to present more difficulties, that I don't believe can be completely solved within the budget of a domestic studio. Still, if you have a tolerant family or friends, a partial improvement may be enough to allow you to continue recording.

FLOATING FLOOR

'Floating floor' is a term you may have heard bandied about in connection with professionally constructed studios. It's really a heavy, false floor mounted on acoustic isolators; it doesn't actually come into direct contact with the walls of the room at any point, and so minimises structurally-borne sound. Often the floor is cast from reinforced concrete, several inches thick, and may be supported over a void several feet deep, the weight being taken by spring or machine rubber mountings, specially designed so that the resonant frequency of the structure is lower than the very lowest notes the monitor system can reproduce.

Even without the generous void space (necessary to prevent air coupling at low frequencies), this type of construction is rarely appropriate for home studio use, as the original floor would need to be immensely strong to support the new floating floor. You'd also lose a significant amount of room height once the floor was in place unless you dug out the original floor and put in new foundations. In practice, only the really serious pro studios go in for such massive floor designs but they are necessary when the internal rooms are to be built of brick or concrete block rather than studding and plasterboard. They are also desirable if the studio is located close to a heavy traffic route, a railway or an underground line.

LIGHTWEIGHT FLOORS

But there are less massive floor designs available. If you feel that you need to install a floating floor, the method described is within the scope of a competent DIY enthusiast and shouldn't be too heavy for a typical domestic floor to support. Because of the much lower mass, this will be less effective than a purpose designed, floating concrete studio floor, but it will certainly be significantly better than relying on underfelt and should improve matters dramatically except at very low frequencies where some leakage will still occur.

The easiest way to make a floating floor is to use a material known as Lamella, a tongued and grooved flooring chipboard backed with a tightly packed Rockwool material specially made so that all the fibres are perpendicular to the board, rather like a giant scrubbing brush. Normally, a hard felt strip would be fitted around the room, rather like a felt skirting board, and the Lamella boards placed directly onto the existing floor so that they butt up against the felt strip rather than being allowed to touch the solid walls. On top of this is laid another layer of standard flooring grade chipboard but with the joints staggered so as to give a rigid floor. The layers are both screwed and glued together.

This type of flooring may also be used as the base to build a studding/plasterboard room-within-a-room type of studio so long as the weight of the inner room isn't so great as to cause the floor to bow under its weight. Figure 4.1 shows how a Lamella floor is fitted.

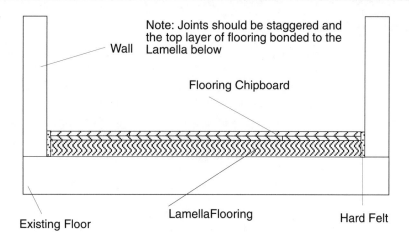

Figure 4.1: Floating Lamella Floor

Alternatively, you can build your own floating floor based on a wooden frame covered in flooring chipboard. Such a floor may be built on a 2x2" or larger timber frame separated from the original floor by blocks of Neoprene, or you could opt to cover the existing floor with two inch Rockwool slab and then lay layers of chipboard directly onto this. Another alternative often used is to rest the frame on pads of insulation board.

By building up two or more layers of chipboard with the joints staggered, a rigid floor can be made that offers a reasonable degree of isolation. Observe the rules on isolation by not allowing the floor to touch the existing walls at any point and fill all gaps with mastic to ensure the structure is airtight. Figure 4.2 illustrates how this may be achieved.

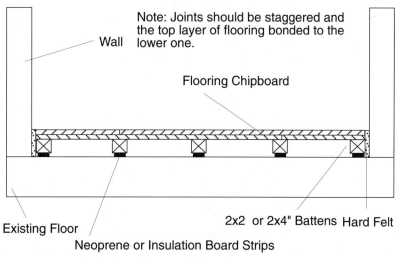

Figure 4.2: Floating Framework Floor

FLOATING RAFT

Alternatively, you could build a floating raft to accommodate your louder instruments such as drums or guitar amplifiers. This is really a section of floating floor, but it's far less heavy than the type of structure a professional studio might use and it doesn't need to cover the entire floor area. It consists simply of layers of 3/4" chipboard nailed or screwed to a frame made from 4x2" joists which then rests on blocks of Neoprene, insulation board or glass fibre in the same way as our DIY floating floor.

Like the true floating floor, it must not touch the walls at any point and you can ensure this by tacking glass fibre, felt or Neoprene strip around the walls of the room or to the edge of your raft. This method won't produce such good results as the complete floor, but it will improve matters noticeably for very little outlay. A further slight improvement can be made by filling the spaces between the joists supporting the raft with glass fibre or Rockwool.

CEILINGS

But what happens if you have someone living above you who is less than enthused with your musical endeavours? You won't keep much sound out by sticking acoustic foam tiles to the ceiling and besides, a proportion of what is heard above passes through the walls and the structure of the house so treating the ceiling on its own isn't going to be a complete cure. In this case, the previously mentioned ploys for isolating noisy equipment from the structure of the building will help. A heavy suspended ceiling might work in a professional studio, but it's less practical to implement than a floating floor in a home environment and many modern rooms lack the necessary height.

But you may not need to go all the way and build a suspended false ceiling, the first step should be to fit underfelt to the room above your studio. Even if this room belongs to someone else, they may be happy to cooperate if you are paying!

The next step is to remove the ceiling plaster or plasterboard from the ceiling to expose the joists. If the floor above is made from conventional floorboards, then the chances are that there will be gaps that need filling. If the problem isn't serious, a mastic gun may be all you need. A more thorough approach is to fit barrier mat between the joists as shown in Figure 4.3. Barrier mat is a mineral loaded plastic material that resembles a heavy, flexible lino and is usually fixed in place using a powered staple gun.

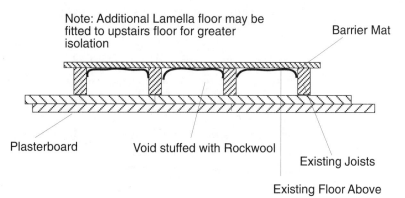

Figure 4.3: Use of Barrier Mat

Once the barrier mat is in place, the gaps between the joists can be stuffed with Rockwool and the underside of the joists covered with two layers of 12mm plasterboard. Again, this is slightly more effective if the surface is plaster skimmed.

SUSPENDED CEILINGS

If you're determined to build a false ceiling, a common approach is outlined in Figure 4.4 but do check with a builder first to ensure that your walls can bear the additional weight. You may also need bigger joists if the room span is larger than average. Notice that the joists for the new ceiling are fixed in between the existing ceiling joists to conserve space. If you have plenty of headroom, this may not be necessary. In any event, the use of barrier mat to seal the floor above is recommended.

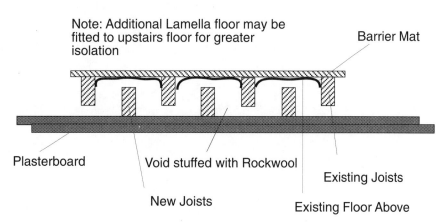

Figure 4.4: Suspended Ceiling

Here, the ceiling is built from joists and plasterboard in much the same way as a partition wall but this time it rests on wooden joists or wall plates fixed to the original walls. The gap between the false ceiling and the original one may be stuffed with Rockwool or glass fibre, and the heavier the false ceiling, the more likely it is to succeed. Once again, use two layers of plasterboard. Some designers also use alternate layers of different material including chipboard, plasterboard and insulation board. You'll notice that this structure isn't isolated from the side wall, but research has shown that, in the case of ceilings, this isn't so important.

Commercial studios may have up to four inches of plasterboard and chipboard hanging over their client's heads but don't be tempted to go to extremes without proper architectural advice.

FLOATING ROOMS

Floating rooms, or shells as they are sometimes called, may sound complicated, but most are based on the same constructional principles as studding walls and floating floors. In other words, they are built on a studding frame which is then covered, outside and in, with layers of plasterboard, chipboard and fibre-board. A top-flight professional studio might use a concrete inner shell built onto a floating concrete floor, but with the increased use of MIDI and an increasing tendency to monitor at lower levels, a lot of pro studios are now being designed with a timber-framed shell.

Either way, the trick is to avoid structurally borne sound which means building the floating room as a free-standing structure supported on a suitable floating floor. For small studios utilising 2x4" wall timbers and 8x2" roof timbers, Lamella flooring is usually adequate - though it should be strengthened by adding at least two layers of flooring chipboard to prevent the floor bowing under the weight of the walls. Figure 5.1 shows the general method of construction, but for clarity, only one layer of additional flooring is shown.

If the width of the inner room is to be greater than 10 to 12 feet, then a central ceiling support will almost certainly be needed and you should seek the advice of a competent builder or architect.

DOORS

Floating rooms should be accessed by double door systems, otherwise all your hard-won sound isolation will be seriously compromised. The door in the existing wall is normally arranged to open outwards while the door in

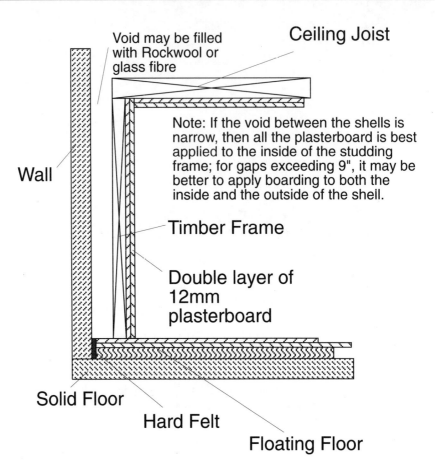

Figure 5.1 General Shell Construction

the floating room opens inwards. Leave a small gap between the frames of the two doors and fill this with mastic to prevent structurally borne sound crossing the void. Expanding foam may also be useful in these areas as it acts as both an adhesive and a gap filler while remaining a poor conductor of sound. However, it is very light and so should only be used to fill small gaps.

If the void between the inner and outer room is small, then it is usual to apply all the plasterboard to the inside face of the inner room so as to maintain as large an air gap as possible between the inner and outer walls. However, if the air gap is larger than 9" or so, then applying plasterboard to both the inner and outer faces of the floating room will give better isolation.

Care must be taken to ensure that the structure is airtight (other than via any properly installed air-conditioning ducts) and potential trouble spots, (aside from the door seals which you already know about), are wherever cables enter the room. It only takes a tiny hole to allow sound to come flooding in, so after the cables have been fitted, seal the entrance points with mastic or expanding foam.

MONITOR ISOLATION

Floating rooms are used both in control room design and in studio design. Control room designs often incorporate non-parallel walls to prevent the build-up of flutter echoes and may also include alcoves for equipment or monitors. It is important when designing for built-in monitors to isolate the monitors from the structure of the floating room or the sound quality will be severely compromised. This is because sound travels faster in solids than it does in air and you can end up in the situation where the structurally borne sound arrives at the engineer's ears before the direct sound from the speakers. If this is allowed to happen, the overall sound quality suffers and the stereo imaging is adversely affected.

A simple way to overcome this is to build a chipboard box on which to sit the monitor and place a neoprene or rubber mat between the bottom of the box and the floor. The speakers may also be decoupled from the box by mounting them on neoprene mats or pads of Blu-Tak.

The box should be filled with dry sand before mounting the speakers - an empty box will simply resonate making the sound worse than ever. The

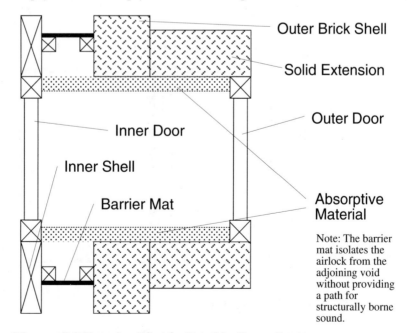

Outer Brick Shell

Solid Extension

Outer Door

Inner Door

Inner Shell

Barrier Mat

Absorptive Material

Note: The barrier mat isolates the airlock from the adjoining void without providing a path for structurally borne sound.

Figure 5.2 Barrier Mat in Double Door System

subject of choosing and installing monitors will be covered in detail later in the book.

WINDOWS

Windows and doors represent weak spots as regards sound isolation, and because the outer building shell is much heavier than the inner room, the doors and windows in this outer shell must be made as heavy as possible. Commercial installations use thick plate glass windows, but standard double-glazing units in both the inner and outer walls also gives good results. Some designers also prefer to isolate the window and door apertures from the the rest of the inter-room void by using barrier mat to build a flexible tunnel around the openings joining the inner and outer walls. Because this material is both heavy and flexible, it does not transmit sound vibrations. This use of barrier mat is illustrated in Figure 5.2.

In a conventional shell-type studio installation comprising a separate studio and control room, leakage between the two rooms can be a problem because of the relatively light structure of the two inner rooms. Simply making the two facing walls heavier is of little help as sound enters the inter-room void via the weakest point. However, it is possible to fix a curtain of barrier mat between the two inner rooms, fixed to battens on the inside of the outer walls, floor and ceiling. This may be

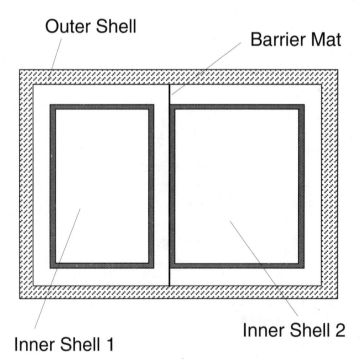

Figure 5.3 Barrier Mat Between Studio and Control Room

stapled directly to the outside of the frame of one of the inner rooms as shown in Figure 5.3

VOIDS

As stated in the introduction, low frequency sound isolation in a double wall structure depends on a large air gap for its efficiency. A gap of several feet is ideal with a gap of around 6" being a practical minimum if a decrease in low-frequency isolation is tolerable. Some designers advocate filling the void with Rockwool though this may not make such a large difference as you might imagine due to its weight being low relative to the surrounding structure.

But even in large studios where generous air gaps are used, these gaps don't have to be wasted space; they can be designed into the plan as corridors, storage spaces, machine rooms or air locks.

ACOUSTIC TREATMENTS

Once the acoustic isolation of a room has been sorted out, it is very unlikely that it will function as a good listening (or performing) room without further treatment. And, to compound matters, there appears to be widespread disagreement as to what constitutes the ideal listening environment. It should be noted at this point that while the control room should be approached with a view to providing the best possible environment in which to listen to and evaluate the music being recorded and mixed, the performing area or studio is likely to have quite different acoustic properties which may be dictated, as much as anything, by current fashion.

In some cases, a relatively dead recording environment is preferred so as to exclude any room ambience; this enables the engineer to start with a clean slate when it it comes to adding artificial effects. On the other hand, most leading engineers and producers would agree that instruments requiring a live acoustic setting invariably sound better in a sympathetic live room than when processed with artificial ambience from a digital reverb unit or echo plate.

Currently a very live room sound is popular for drums or other instruments, and this can be achieved using an absolutely untreated stone or tiled room with an exposed concrete or wooden floor. On the other hand, some instruments record better in a more subdued environment, so it's not uncommon to find playing areas which are live at one end but damped at the other. This should not be confused with live end/dead end control rooms which will be discussed later. Another popular approach is to build a live performing area which can be damped down with movable screens, carpets or drapes. The pros and cons of these various methods will be explored later.

LISTENING ENVIRONMENT

The studio control room is so called because it is supposed to be a controlled environment in which valid musical decisions can be taken. However, because of the multiplicity of different monitor speaker systems in common usage and the widely differing design philosophies of control rooms, the aim of creating some sort of universal standard has yet to be realised. Indeed, it has been said that if you were to take a cross-section of the domestic rooms in which we listen to our stereos and radios, the results would be far more consistent than a survey of so-called studio control rooms. Nevertheless, some agreement on the basic parameters is in evidence so we may as well start there.

ROOM PARAMETERS

First of all, what major factors affect the way a room sounds - and why does the room affect the sound at all for that matter? It's all to do with the fact that sound bounces or reflects off solid surfaces, so we don't just hear the direct sound from our monitor loudspeakers, (or in the studio, the direct sound from the instruments), we also hear a whole series of short echoes as the sound bounces around the room. This series of echoes is better known as reverberation or ambience, though in a good listening room, the reverb time may be too short to be perceptible. What's more, different materials and structures reflect different parts of the audio spectrum more efficiently than others, so the reverb we hear is 'coloured'.

The ideal listening room needs a little reverb to help increase the perceived loudness of the monitors and also to prevent the room sounding unnaturally dead, but the reverb time also needs to be roughly equal at all frequencies across the audio spectrum if colouration is to be avoided. Reverb times of between 0.3 and 0.5 seconds are normally chosen for control rooms, though it is usual for the very low bass reverb time to be slightly longer except in very sophisticated designs where elaborate bass trapping techniques have been employed.

An even reverberation time can only be achieved by the careful deployment of different types of absorbing material and absorbing structures, but even then, too rigorous a mathematical approach is likely to be misleading because of variables such as the materials themselves, reflective and resonant studio equipment introduced after the design is complete, and the presence of people in the studio.

Furthermore, because much of today's actual recording is done in the control room rather than in the studio proper, the design may be a compromise between ergonomics and acoustics.

MODES

To start the ball rolling, we have to take into account room modes which are directly related to room dimensions. These affect both control room and studio acoustics - it's the same set of physical laws. If a sound wave is generated with exactly the same length as the longest dimension of a room, it will be reflected back and forth from the facing walls in phase with the original, thus reinforcing it; this phenomena is known as a standing wave. Accepting the value for the speed of sound as being roughly 1100ft per second, an 11ft room would correspond to one wavelength at 100Hz.

Any music signal played in the room would, therefore, undergo an artificial reinforcement or colouration of sounds at or around 100Hz, but that's not all. Two whole wavelengths at 200Hz also fit neatly into 11ft and three at 300Hz which will also cause standing waves, so we have a potential trouble spot for every 100Hz increase in frequency. And that's only considering one room dimension.

The width and height can be considered in the same way and give rise to their own series of standing wave frequencies, and, because they are related to the three axes of the room - length, width and height - they are called axial modes. There are other more complex modes caused by sound bouncing off more than one wall to make a round trip and these are known as the tangential and oblique modes. But because the sound has to encounter more surfaces to produce these modes, the intensity of the modal peaks is less than the peaks caused by the axial modes.

OPTIMUM DIMENSIONS

Every room has its modes because every room has dimensions, so what's to be done? Research indicates that the best sounding rooms are those where the modes are fairly evenly distributed so that there are no drastic peaks or dips in the low frequency reverberation characteristics of the room. Before attempting to beat any tiresome modes into submission by using absorbers, it is possible to arrive at certain ratios of room dimensions that will minimise the problem of modal resonances.

Consider firstly a room that is exactly the wrong shape: a cube. Here all three axial modes will occur at the same frequencies and so will reinforce each other to form very noticeable peaks in the room response. Non-cuboid shapes are better suited but if, say, one dimension is exactly twice one of the others, then modes can still pile up at certain frequencies causing substantial colouration. Even apparently unrelated dimensions can cause modal pile-ups at some frequencies and much work has been done in the past to find sets of ratios that minimise these undesirable peaks. Large gaps between modes are also a problem and you might find that musical notes falling in these gaps sound dead compared with the rest of the spectrum, rather like the dead spots that occur on some guitars at certain notes.

Above about 300Hz, the modes become so closely spaced that we don't need to worry unduly about peaks or gaps, but below this frequency, we should aim for no gaps between modes of more than 20Hz and no closely packed or coincident modes. This is no easy task - and if our control room is below a certain minimum size, it's impossible. The modal response that we are considering here is arrived at by plotting all three axial modes on the same diagram but ignoring the tangential and oblique modes. There is work where attempts have been made to include these in the calculations too, but the practical results seldom bear out the mathematical predictions. Figure 6.1 shows how the axial modes may be calculated for

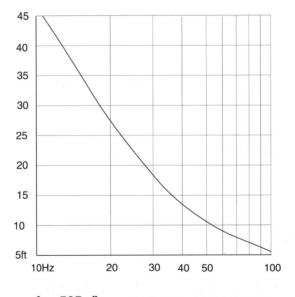

$f_0 = 565n/L$ where L is the distance between opposing surfaces in feet, fo is the frequency of the mode, and n the order of the mode (1,2,3 etc.)

Figure 6.1 Relationship Between Modal Frequencies and Room Dimensions.

each opposing pair of surfaces in a room. By substituting the numbers 1,2,3 and so on for the value of n, a whole series of modes can be calculated, though the most significant are those falling below 300Hz.

BOLT'S GRAPH

Because you will probably not want to spend hours with a calculator, Figure 6.2 shows a very useful graph compiled by Bolt (who presented a paper on the subject in 1946) where the shaded space denotes acceptable room ratios. Even this isn't foolproof though, as some 2:1 room ratios fall into Bolt's area so some care has to be exercised. Several sets of preferred ratios have evolved which work well practically as well as theoretically, three of which are 1 : 1.14 : 1.39, 1 : 1.28 : 1.54 and 1 : 1.6 : 2.33.

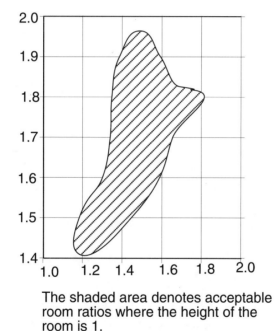

The shaded area denotes acceptable room ratios where the height of the room is 1.

Figure 6.2 Preferred Ratios of Room Dimensions.

It is a common misconception that building non-parallel walls will improve the standing wave situation but sadly, this isn't the case at low frequencies. The low frequency modes will develop much as before. However, it is true that splaying the walls by as little as 1 in 10 or even 1 in 20 will help to diffuse higher frequencies and minimise flutter echoes causes by mid and high frequency sounds bouncing between two facing walls or floor and ceiling.

One architectural feature to avoid at all costs, particularly in your control room, is any form of concave structure such as a bay window or curved wall. These have a nasty habit of focusing reflected sound into one place which plays havoc with the room's acoustic performance. Convex or irregular surfaces on the other hand are generally considered to be desirable features as they tend to diffuse high frequencies leading to a more even sound field.

ADAPTATION

These points are all well and good if you have the option of changing any of your room dimensions, but if the room is already built, you can only lower the ceiling by way of adjustment and even that may be impractical. Don't despair though, for pop or rock music, the actual studio size and shape isn't quite so critical. There's a lot of close miking employed and much of the sound subscribes more to fashion rather than to pure fidelity. It's in speech work such as drama or music involving acoustic instruments that well behaved acoustics are most important in the actual studio area.

Equally, an apparently problematic control room can usually be made workable by choosing appropriate monitors and mounting them in a suitable position.

ABSORBERS

Having introduced the leading rogues when it comes to acoustic design work, it's now time to check out some of our allies. Absorbing mid and high frequencies is not much of a problem, there are several proprietary acoustic tiles, foams and heavy drapes that can effectively soak up frequencies above 300Hz and even humble carpet has its uses, but the bass end requires more tenacity.

The reason for this is that low frequency sounds have long wavelengths and a purely absorptive bass trap needs to be at least one eighth of a wavelength deep to do any good. At 50Hz, that's approaching three feet and there aren't many studios that can afford the space to cover one or more walls with a three foot thickness of Rockwool. However, this type of trap has the advantage of working equally well at all frequencies down to its lower cutoff point.

The other, and understandably more popular, approach is to build a damped resonant structure that will absorb a significant proportion of a specific frequency band by converting it to heat via frictional losses. As the sound energy expended by a Wembley football crowd during a complete FA cup match, including overtime, would barely be sufficient to warm a pot of tea for the teams at half time, you have no need to worry about thrash metal bands setting fire to your walls during over-zealous solos!

RESONANT TRAPS

There are two commonly used traps both of which are easy to build: the panel absorber and the Helmholz resonator. Both take up a large area but have the advantage of being only a few inches deep rather than several feet. Even so, you must bear in mind that these are tuned traps and so are normally used to reduce specific resonances - they are not suitable for use as broadband absorbers with the exception of a panel trap constructed with a highly damped, limp membrane.

PANEL ABSORBER

The panel absorber is the easiest and most predictable bass trap to design and build, consisting of a simple wooden frame over which is fixed a thin, flexible panel such as plywood, hardboard or roofing felt. Fibreglass or Rockwool is fixed inside the frame to help absorb the low frequency energy. The resonant frequency is a function of cavity depth and mass per square foot of the panel material, so it's easy to calculate the dimensions.

The actual area doesn't make any significant difference to the operating frequency, but obviously the more you want to reduce the low frequency reverberation time, the larger the area of panel you'll need in any given room. To better understand the effect of a given area of absorber, consider that a perfectly efficient full-range trap will affect the sound in the same was as an open window of the same size, but without the associated problems of sound leakage.

The formula is: $F = 170/\sqrt{M \times D}$ where F is the frequency you're aiming to absorb, M is the mass of the panel in lbs per square foot and D is the depth of the air space in inches.

The metric equivalent is; $F = 60/\sqrt{M \times D}$ where the mass is in kilograms and the unit of length is metres.

Filling the cavity with fibreglass or mineral wool tends to lower the resonant frequency by up to 50% and can double the effectiveness of the trap. It also lowers the Q of the trap so that it is effective over a wider frequency range. A typical panel-type trap is effective for frequencies around one octave either side of the centre frequency, so you don't have to be deadly accurate to get results.

Higher frequencies may be reflected from the surface and curved panel traps have been constructed to simultaneously absorb bass frequencies and diffuse higher ones. Figure 6.3 shows the constructional details of a conventional panel absorber. It is permissible to cover the front face of the trap with acoustic foam to extend its usefulness to the mid and high end of the audio spectrum.

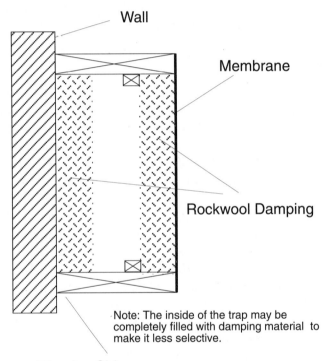

Figure 6.3 Panel Absorber.

DAMPING

An undamped panel trap using a rigid membrane will radiate some energy back into the room after the incident sound has ceased - clearly an undesirable state of affairs, and so some degree of damping is generally included. Though panel traps are normally considered to be tuned absorbers, the use of a heavy, well damped panel material lowers the Q of the trap so much that it may be considered a broad band device, especially when combined with plenty of internal damping.

There are specialist materials such as mineral loaded vinyl or even lead loaded materials that are heavy, flexible and highly damped which lend themselves to wide band bass trap design. Excellent results can be also obtained from a Rockwool filled trap, between eight and twelve inches deep, with a simple roofing felt membrane. The sides may also be fitted with felt membranes instead of being left solid in order to increase the absorbent area presented to the room.

With such a high degree of damping, the action of the trap is less like a resonant panel and more like a floppy wall - the sound energy is expended in trying to vibrate the felt which is so well damped that the energy is largely absorbed. Because the Q of such traps is low, the depth of the trap becomes far less critial.

Many historic buildings feature wood panelling and these often have well controlled acoustical properties. That's because a panelled wall with an air space behind acts as a tuned bass absorber. To a lesser extent, studio construction involving plasterboard fixed to a frame also helps us in that it acts, to some extent, as a trap for bass and mid frequencies. In practical terms, that makes it easier to treat a room that has a lightweight construction than one that is solid because a large proportion of the bass energy passes straight through the walls instead of being reflected back. Unfortunately, what is helpful as regards acoustic treatment is, in this case, totally at odds with what is desirable for good sound isolation unless you are dealing with a lightweight inner shell built within a solid outer shell.

HELMHOLZ TRAPS

The Helmholz resonator works on the same principle as blowing over the neck of a bottle to obtain a tone. A bottle has a very narrow bandwidth but by introducing an absorbent material such as fibreglass or mineral wool into the neck to reduce the Q, the operating range can be widened. You don't see many studios full of bottles (at least not used as bass traps) but you do see perforated panels which may be either bass or mid traps depending on how they are tuned.

By fixing a perforated wooden panel over a frame and putting an absorbent material inside the box, a resonant bass trap is formed. A simple formula can be applied to determine the operating frequency.

$$R = 200 \sqrt{P/DT}$$

R is the resonant frequency, P is the percentage of perforation (total hole area divided by panel area times 100), T is the effective hole depth in inches (thickness of panel plus 0.8 of the hole diameter) and D is the depth of the air space in inches.

Figure 6.4 shows the construction of the Helmholz trap. By varying the perforation percentage, the design can be applied to both the bass and mid range. Predicting the performance of these traps, however, is difficult because the Q or bandwidth depends on the amount of internal damping.

The other problem is getting the right perforation percentage. Common pegboard is usually used in mid traps rather than bass traps. For example,

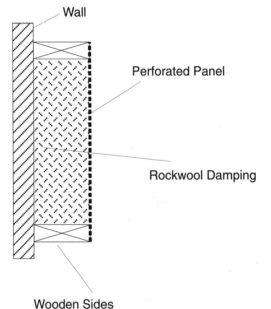

Wall

Perforated Panel

Rockwool Damping

Wooden Sides

Figure 6.4 Perforated Helmholtz-type Absorber.

pegboard having 3/16" holes on a 1" matrix has a perforation percentage of 2.75%. Fixed over a 4" air gap, this gives a resonant frequency of a little over 400Hz. Boards of different perforation percentages are available from specialist acoustic suppliers but are not readily available from conventional builders' supply merchants.

Like the panel absorber, adding an absorbent material lowers the resonant frequency slightly and broadens the resonant peak. Instead of using perforated board, it's theoretically possible to use a series of slats to create the correct slot percentage rather than individual holes, but apparently the calculations for such an absorber are likely to be at odds with the result unless they are quite involved. Helmholz resonators were once very widely used in both broadcast and recording studios but panel traps with limp membranes seem more widespread in modern designs.

MID AND HIGH ABSORBERS

One of the simplest absorbers for use at higher frequencies is simple open-cell foam such as that used in furniture. For safety reasons, the fire-retardant type should be used and expensive acoustic foam tiles are often only sculpted versions of this same material. The lowest frequency that will be effectively absorbed is dictated by the thickness of the foam, a 1" foam being most effective above 1kHz while a 4" foam is useful down to 250Hz. The low frequency absorption can also be improved by spacing the foam away from the wall by a few inches on a wooden frame.

A similar absorber can be made from 2" Rockwool slab, fixed to a frame two inches away from the wall and covered with open-weave fabric to prevent the fibres escaping into the air. Again, this should be usefully effective down to 250Hz or so.

Carpet is insufficiently thick to be effective at anything less than the high frequency end of the spectrum and its absorbency drops off noticeably below 2kHz. There is a slight advantage to using a foam-backed carpet, and once again, mounting this with an airspace behind will extend its effectiveness down another octave or so.

Variable absorbency in the mid and high frequency range can be achieved by hanging heavy drapes a few inches from the wall. These should be generous enough to allow the material to hang in folds rather than being stretched tightly, and if these are hung on a rail in front of a reflective surface, it's a simple matter to draw back the drapes to convert a dead acoustic into a live one.

MOVABLE SCREENS

Portable acoustic screens are useful because they can be used to modify the sound of a small part of a room for the recording of, say, a vocal track, drums or acoustic guitar. These screens are generally built with a polished wood or synthetic laminate face on one side and a Rockwool or foam absorber about four inches thick on the other. They are supported by simple wooden legs and, by facing either the hard or the absorbent side to the performer, either a live or dead environment is created. These screens are only effective down to around 250Hz on their absorbent side but that's usually adequate.

Drum booths may be set up using a set of tall screens with another screen balanced on the top to form a roof. To aid eye contact, some screens are built with thick perspex windows in them. For drums, acoustic guitars and so on, the live side is normally used, and for vocals, the dead side. Figure 6.5 shows how a simple acoustic screen may be constructed.

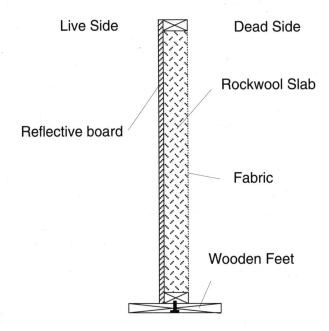

Figure 6.5 Simple Acoustic Screen

DESIGN CRITERIA

Acoustic treatment is primarily concerned with absorbing sound with the ultimate aim of producing an even reverberation time across the audio spectrum and a mean decay time that falls within acceptable limits for the application in hand. Treatments may also be devised for the diffusion or scattering of sound in order to further randomise the reflections arriving at the listener.

Most of us will be familiar with reverberation both as an artificial and as a natural effect. It occurs in all normal rooms to the extent that music or speech sounds unnatural without it, but in a studio control room environment, the reverberation characteristics need to be controlled within fairly close limits if the end product is to be evaluated with any accuracy.

Reverberation is created whenever sound energy is fed into a room and the room modes are excited. When the source of energy is removed, the reverberation will decay at a rate determined by the geometry and absorbency of the room and its contents. Excessive low frequency reverberation related to one dominating mode can cause serious problems as the room will appear to be bass heavy at this frequency.

If this is allowed to occur in a studio control room, the danger is that you may attempt to correct your mix using EQ to cure the bass boost, but then when you play your mix on a properly balanced hi-fi system, the result sounds bass light. Furthermore, excessive reverb time at one frequency can cause notes to hang on after they should have finished playing which leads to a general lack of definition.

T60

Reverberation time (RT) is defined as the time taken for a sound to die away to one thousandth of its original sound pressure. This is more commonly called T60 as the reverb time is measured after the sound has decayed by 60dB. The decay in sound energy follows an exponential curve and the ideal reverb time varies depending on the room size and the type of material being auditioned. For speech, the optimum reverb time is generally agreed to be somewhere between 0.2S and 0.5S, whereas music might require between 0.6S and 0.8S of reverberation. A typical living room has a T60 of around 0.5S and that's not a bad figure to aim for in your control room.

Problems arise because the T60 tends to be different at different frequencies and this brings up the question of whether we should strive in our studio design to achieve the same RT at all frequencies or whether we should accept the longer T60 at lower frequencies produced by a typical furnished room. Many arguments have been provoked by this question, but the current consensus seems to be that for small listening rooms such as studios, we should aim for as constant a reverb time as possible over the whole audio spectrum, or at least up to 7-8kHz. Even so, for home studios or small professional studios not using monitoring systems with a very deep bass response, a slight rise of RT at lower frequencies is permissible.

PRAGMATISM

Designing the acoustics of a control room using mathematical principles is more than a little involved, and the variable nature of many of the key parameters makes it unlikely that the end result will correlate with the calculated figures. Even so, a mathematical treatment will at least get you into the right ball park. If the thought of wading through a load of calculations fills you with foreboding, don't worry because there are several approaches to acoustic design that can be applied by following very general and well proven principles, and these will be covered later.

Though the results of such a non-rigorous approach might be less than satisfactory when designing a large, professional control room intended for use with a powerful, full-range monitoring system, you'll almost certainly find that you can create a suitable listening environment for home recording or for a small commercial facility by adhering to a few simple guidelines.

This is possible because the smaller monitors used in such studios don't have such an extended bass as the very large monitors used in large commercial installations, and so there is less low frequency energy produced to excite the room where its T60 is longer than might be desirable. Additionally, smaller monitors can be used closer to the engineer and so the ratio of direct and reflected sound is higher meaning that the room acoustics have less effect on the perceived sound.

But, for the benefit of those bent on the task of working the whole thing out on paper first, the underlying principles follow:

SABINE

The mathematics needed to calculate reverb time or T60 are fairly straightforward if we rely on the formula devised by Sabine. There is a more accurate but far more complicated approach pioneered by Eyring but as the end result never quite agrees with the calculations anyway, Sabine is plenty good enough. Sabine states that:

$$T60 = \frac{0.05 \times V}{ST \times Aave}$$

where T60 is the reverb time in seconds, V is the volume of the room in cubic feet, ST is the total surface area of the room in square feet and Aave is the average absorption coefficient of the surfaces within the room. If the room is to be furnished, these areas, volumes and materials should be included in the calculations. It's possible to obtain a table of absorption coefficients relating to all the commonly used building, decorating and furnishing materials, but a few of the more useful ones gleaned from various textbooks are included at the end of this chapter.

The metric equivalent of this formula is:

$$RT = \frac{0.161 \times V}{ST \times Aave}$$

where the volume is measured in cubic metres, and the surface area in square metres.

ABSORPTION UNITS

Multiplying the total surface area of the room by the average absorption coefficient gives us the total number of absorption units in the room and these units are called Sabines. This unit is handy because we can look at each section of surface separately, calculate the number of Sabines it contributes, and then add up all the Sabines for the room to give us the bottom line for our simple equation. For example, the absorption coefficient for concrete at 125Hz is about 0.01 which isn't very high. 500 square feet of concrete surface such as a floor would give us 500x0.01 = 5 Sabines of absorption. Add on the Sabines due to plaster walls, carpeted floor, panel absorbers or whatever and you end up with the total number of Sabines for the room at 125Hz.

To complicate the issue slightly, the absorption coefficient for a given material, you will remember, varies with frequency so the tables give us six different values at one octave intervals from 125Hz through to 4kHz. And that means working through the formula six times with six sets of values to give us six T60 times, one for each octave. What we then have to do is to isolate areas of the audio spectrum where there is too little or too much absorption and then pencil in a trap, a carpet or a few acoustic tiles and then go through it all again to see if things are better. Anyone capable of writing even simple computer programs in Basic or using a spreadsheet should be able to automate this tedious calculation, but a simple calculator is quite adequate.

One limitation of Sabine's equation is that it assumes a perfectly diffused soundfield, which most small rooms don't have, and it also ignores any sound absorption by the air itself. Hence, any result arrived at on this basis should be treated as a guide rather than as a proven fact. Acoustic consultants make a good living out of weighing these calculations against reality, holding their finger in the wind and then coming up with a solution that works.

DISTRIBUTION

It is good practice to try to balance the properties of facing walls rather than calculate that you need X amount of trapping for the whole room and then stick it all in one place. For example, if the floor is carpeted, it will absorb the higher frequencies very efficiently but will hardly affect the bass at all. One answer might be to mount bass traps in the ceiling to absorb the bass but to reflect back the mid and higher frequencies.

The techniques are the same for the studio area as for the control room, though you may decide on a different T60 for the studio as discussed earlier. Furthermore, the control room calculations should take into account the reflective surfaces of equipment and windows and the room must be as acoustically symmetrical as possible. There are so many different philosophies on control room design from LEDE (Live End Dead End) to padded cells that there's a separate chapter on that topic later in the book. The only real criteria is that the room should be conducive to creating mixes that the record buying public wish to buy, anything else is purely academic.

DOING THE SUMS

Firstly, check your rooms' dimensions to see if they fall inside Bolt's area; if not, you might like to plot out your main room modes and find out where trouble spots are likely to occur so you can employ some extra trapping if necessary. Next, decide very carefully on what floor covering is to be used as this will have a significant effect due to the large area involved. If you design your room for a vinyl floor, you can't change it to carpet later on without going back to square one and changing everything else. At this point, you could invoke Sabine and work out the T60s for the room as it stands at 125Hz, 250Hz, 500Hz, 1kHz, 2kHz and 4kHz which will probably reveal an excessively long T60 at 125Hz.

After that it's back to the drawing pad and, with the help of Sabine and a table of absorption coefficients, you should be able to arrive at the areas of treatment you need to get your T60 close to your target figure at all six frequencies. The best way to do this is to calculate how many Sabines you need to provide at each frequency and work from there. It's then a matter of taking into account the available surfaces which are not occupied by doors, shelves, windows, equipment and suchlike to distribute your acoustic absorbers.

This procedure sounds more complicated than it is, but I won't say that it isn't time consuming and more than a little frustrating, though it needs to be done only once for each room. But however careful your calculations, please remember that the result is only going to be an approximation due to the limitations of Sabine's equation when applied to small rooms and also the uncertain absorption coefficients of various materials. Listening or specialised measurement is the only way to tell if you have a successful result.

FLUTTER ECHO

Flutter echo is a distinctive ringing sound caused by echoes bouncing back and forth between hard, parallel surfaces following a percussive sound such as a hand clap. To minimise flutter echoes which can plague even a studio having a perfect T60 across the band, certain precautions should be taken. Ideally, facing walls should be out of parallel by at least 1 in 10, but if this isn't possible, some form of mid/high absorber can be applied to one or both walls to reduce the problem. Also, some of the absorbers we have discussed such as the panel trap, the Helmholz resonator and the slatted absorber have flat surfaces which are reflective at mid and high frequencies. Consequently, when positioning these, it is a good idea not to have them facing each other across a parallel room, but to offset them.

Alternatively, traps can be constructed with a sloping surface, where the average depth is maintained by making the half-way depth equal to the calculated value. Padded door surfaces can also be beneficial and one of the popular methods is to fit 2" of foam to the door covered with upholstery quality vinyl or fabric, fixed by tacks to give a quilted appearance.

USEFUL ABSORPTION COEFFICIENTS

Material	125Hz	250Hz	500Hz	1kHz	2kHz	4kHz
Cotton Drapes draped to half area. 15oz/sq yd						
	0.07	0.37	0.49	0.81	0.65	0.54
Heavy carpet on concrete						
	0.02	0.06	0.14	0.37	0.6	0.65
Coarse concrete						
	0.36	0.44	0.31	0.29	0.39	0.25
Painted concrete						
	0.01	0.05	0.06	0.07	0.09	0.08
Wood floor						
	0.15	0.11	0.10	0.07	0.06	0.07

Window glass

0.35	0.25	0.18	0.12	0.07	0.04

Plate Glass

0.18	0.06	0.04	0.03	0.02	0.02

Plaster on brick

0.013	0.015	0.02	0.03	0.04	0.05

LF panel absorber

0.28	0.22	0.17	0.09	0.10	0.11

Perforated Helmholz absorber using 4" depth with mineral wool damping, 0.79% perforation.

0.4	0.84	0.4	0.16	0.14	0.12

Perforated Helmholz absorber using 8" depth with mineral wool damping, 0.79% perforation.

0.98	0.88	0.52	0.21	0.16	0.14

Broadband absorber consisting of 1" fibreglass slab at mouth of 7" deep cavity

0.67	0.98	0.98	0.93	0.98	0.96

CONTROL ROOM DESIGN

Though the playing area of a studio may be constructed in order to help produce a fashionable sound, the primary aim of a control room is to help the engineer and producer make accurate judgments on the sound being fed through the monitor system. Most rooms not designed with this specific purpose in mind inflict their own character on any sounds occurring in that room, to varying degrees, making accurate evaluation difficult or at worst, impossible. As usual, most of the problems can be attributed to our old friend reverberation which combines with the direct sound from the loudspeakers, often to paint a quite different picture.

In order to minimise the detrimental effects of reverb, we must control the reverb decay time of the studio so that it falls within acceptable limits, and also ensure that the decay time is essentially similar for audio frequencies of up to at least 7kHz.

DIMENSIONS

We've already covered room dimensions, so if you're starting with an empty room, consult Bolt's graph to see how you stand. Most importantly, check that no dimension is an exact multiple of either of the other two as this is likely to lead to trouble This should ensure that the normal modes of the room are distributed fairly evenly and there will be no severe mode pile-ups to cause severe peaks or dips in the room response.

This is less true with small rooms than it is with large ones, and if your control room is smaller than 20ft by 15ft, then the modes will be too widely spaced to be completely even. Even so, by choosing the right type of monitor system and positioning it correctly, the room can still be made to work very well.

If you are planning to build a room-within-a room, then it's worth bearing in mind that very low frequencies will pass through the inner shell and so it's the dimensions of the original room that will prevail below 100Hz or so when it comes to mode creation.

Space permitting, it is desirable to taper the inner shell towards the front of the room and if possible, angle the ceiling upwards towards the rear of

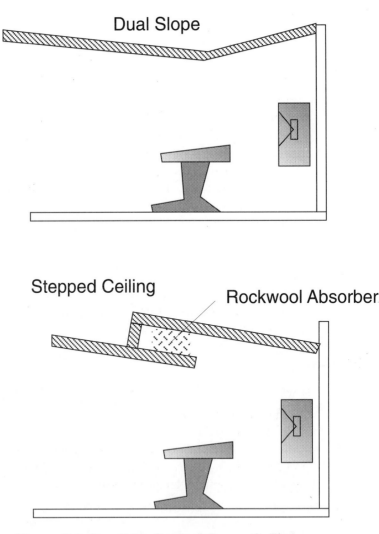

Figure 8.1: Possible Control Room Ceiling Geometries

the room by around one foot in ten. If you can't afford the headroom to do this in one go, you can incorporate multiple slopes. Figure 8.1 shows two possible approaches to ceiling design, the second incorporating a trap to absorb monitor reflections from the front section of the ceiling.

It may help when planning your control room geometry to imagine the walls and ceiling of your room as mirrors and the speakers as light sources; you have to do your best to position everything so you can't see any reflections from your normal engineering position. And remember that your mixing console, equipment racks and any doors or windows are also going to act as mirrors.

TARGET REVERB TIME

It is usual to have a shorter reverberation time in the control room than in the studio in order that the control room reverb doesn't mask any ambience effects taking place in the studio, but again there's some disagreement as to the ideal time. Estimates range from less than 0.2S to as much as 0.8S, but you could reasonably ask why we allow any reverberation at all? If the sound coming over the monitors has already had reverb artificially added, should it not then be heard in a totally dead room? After all, there's no room reverb on headphones.

ANECHOIC ROOMS

There are two problems with the completely dead or anechoic approach. One is simply that the human ear and brain system does not like to work in an anechoic environment. Some reflected sound is needed to fulfil what must be a psychological need. Possibly confusion arises from the fact that the eye is telling the brain that it's in an enclosed room while the ear is claiming to be outdoors on a very quiet day.

The second of the two problems is somewhat less metaphysical; a pair of speakers driving into an anechoic room will produce far less sound level than the same speaker system in a room with reflective surfaces. We all know how important loud monitoring seems to be, so the solution is again a compromise, especially as the most accurate monitors currently available are not as loud as some of the less accurate but more efficient systems.

In defence of the anechoic room, it does offer a listening environment where we hear only the direct, on-axis sound from the monitors. As most speakers perform less well off-axis than on-axis, the reverberant field of a typical listening room is further coloured by the off-axis characteristics of the monitors. But in an anechoic room, all off-axis sound is absorbed and so never reaches the listener. This environment is, however, quite unlike that in which the final record is likely to be played.

PHILOSOPHY

Most acoustic engineers tend to agree that to monitor a stereo recording satisfactorily, we need a room that is acoustically symmetrical about an axis bisecting the speaker positions and running through to the mid point of the rear wall. This means applying equal amounts of absorbent materials to opposite walls and balancing any reflective surfaces created by windows, doors or equipment with similar reflectors opposite. It is here that splayed walls come into play, because if we were to make the room acoustically symmetrical and have parallel walls, we would be setting up the ideal conditions to generate flutter echoes.

It is also generally agreed that the speakers should be set up along the longest wall of the studio. The reason for this is that the most intrusive sound reflections are those emanating from the side walls, and by arranging the room so the side walls are as far away as possible, the problem is minimised. The actual positioning of speakers will be discussed in the chapter on monitors.

Some designers advocate distributing absorbent materials in patches along the walls so that no two patches of identical treatment are facing each other but are slightly staggered. Most pundits would, again, tend to agree, but where they start to shake their heads is when it comes to discussing whether the front of the room should be more live than the back, the back more live than the front or the absorbent materials equally distributed around the studio. There are convincing arguments for choosing any of the three approaches.

LIVE OR DEAD?

If we construct a studio which has equally absorbent walls, then the stereo imaging will be good, because there are no concentrations of reflections from any particular source to confuse the ear, but by the same token, the subjective sound is not very loud and the stereo image fairly narrow. This uniformly absorbent philosophy was widely used in control room for many years, and in many ways still makes sense as domestic listening rooms tend to have the absorbent surfaces scattered around rather than being concentrated in one place.

If, on the other hand, we make the rear of the room dead and leave the front live, we will get a lot of strong early reflections from the walls close to the speakers which will make it hard to pinpoint the position of any specific sound in the mix and may introduce colourations. On the positive side though, this gives an impressively wide sound and is subjectively loud which means that the monitors don't have to work quite so hard. Proponents of this style of control room argue that providing you have a lot of closely spaced early reflections, the subjective sound quality isn't unduly affected - it's when you have just a few really strong reflections that the real problems start.

Studios following this design philosophy tend to employ soffit mounting speakers surrounded by sloped, reflective surfaces in order to make sure that the first early reflections really do follow the original sound very closely.

The third option approaches the currently popular LEDE (Live End, Dead End) concept and by making the front of the room dead but leaving the back live, we tighten up the imaging yet still manage to achieve a fair subjective loudness due to the reflections from the rear wall reinforcing the sound. Off-axis monitor reflections are reduced, yet the rear of the room is live enough to permit normal conversation.

To understand the implications of this arrangement, we must refer back to the theories of Haas, who investigated the effects of adding a delayed version of a signal to itself.

HAAS EFFECT

If the delay time is less than around 50mS, then the delay merges with the original sound and the brain treats the result as a single sound. The actual time varies from person to person, but 50mS will do fine for the sake of argument. If, however, the delay is longer, the brain picks out the original sound and focuses on it while attaching less significance to the reflections allowing us to concentrate better on the original sound.

LEDE

In the Live End Dead End studio, absorbent material at the front of the studio, combined with clever geometry, virtually eliminates these early reflections falling inside Haas's 50mS window and produces instead, longer delays due to the fact that the direct sound has to travel all the way to the back of the room before it encounters a surface that can bounce it back to the listening position.

Consequently, these reflections do not obscure the engineer's perception of the direct sound so much, but they do contribute to the overall perception of loudness while satisfying the psychological need for reflected sound. Another advantage of eliminating early reflections in the control room is that sounds miked up in the actual studio invariably contain a degree of reverberation caused by room ambience. In a LEDE studio, this detail is not masked by early reflections in the control room.

Note that to ensure the rear reflections fall outside the Haas window, the control room would need to be at least 25 feet from front to back common enough in top-end pro studios, but less practical in smaller facilities or home recording setups.

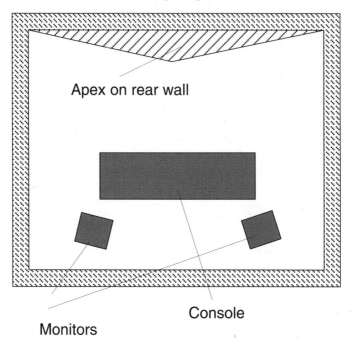

Figure 8.2: Control room, showing Apex Diffuser

DIFFUSION

There is more to a good LEDE design, though, than simply deadening the first third or half of the room and geometry has just as important a part to play as the choice of absorbers. It is also desirable to break up or diffuse reflections coming from the rear wall, something that must be taken into account when building or altering the room. Bear in mind previous comments on this subject and don't be tempted to make the rear wall concave; this will focus the sound into one spot, making it impossible to hear the same mix in any two parts of the room.

A practical approach is to incorporate convex surfaces into the rear wall design such as sections of cylinders, or even to bring the centre of the wall a couple of feet out into the room in the form of an apex as shown in Figure 8.2. Shelves of equipment also help to diffuse the sound - a good cost-effective treatment for the home studio.

LEDE LIMITATIONS

Even if you deaden all available front surfaces with highly efficient absorbers, there are reflections from the control room window glass, from the surface of the console and from any equipment that happens to be close by. Also the floor is unlikely to absorb much in the way of low frequencies. This is where careful geometry pays off in ensuring that as few reflections as possible are directed back at the engineer's listening position. If you consider the loudspeakers as light sources and the reflective surfaces as mirrors, you should be able to visualise the most direct sound reflection paths keeping in mind that the angle of incidence always equals the angle of reflection.

Despite the problems in making a room behave exactly as LEDE theory dictates, the approach does yield good results and is currently much in

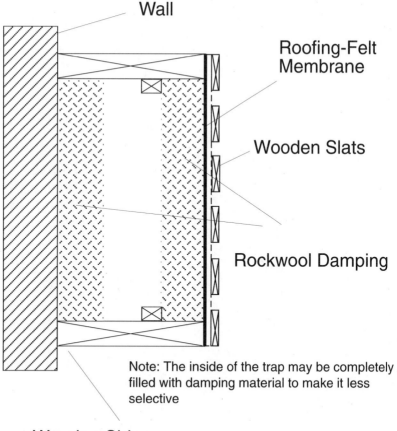

Wall

Roofing-Felt Membrane

Wooden Slats

Rockwool Damping

Note: The inside of the trap may be completely filled with damping material to make it less selective

Wooden Sides

Figure 8.3: Combined Diffuser and Bass Trap

favour. Many modern control rooms lean towards the LEDE philosophy, though the best description of the majority might be 'Livish End, Deadish End'!

TRAPPING

Mid and high frequency absorption is easily handled by appropriately deployed Rockwool, acoustic foam or drapes as described in earlier chapters, but the bass end also needs to be considered and some degree of trapping is invariably necessary with all but the smallest monitoring system. The usual approach is to use a deep cavity filled with Rockwool slab or to use a highly damped panel absorber with a roofing felt or specialist, highly damped panel material. These are often incorporated into the rear wall of the studio or at the front around the monitors and control room window. If space allows, additional bass trapping may be built into the ceiling.

It is also possible to combine either the panel-type or Rockwool absorber trap with a rear wall diffuser; the original apex shape is still fine but instead of being covered by solid boarding, it may be filled with Rockwool slab (with or without a roofing felt membrane) and covered with wooden slats spaced apart by an inch or so. For best diffusion, the slat widths and

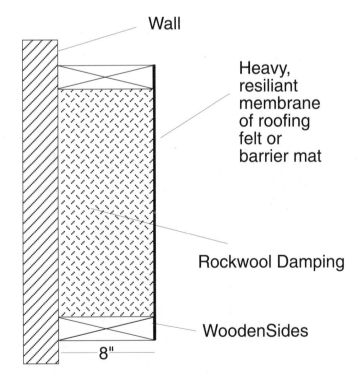

Figure 8.4: Shallow, Wide-Range Trap

spacings should be irregular. Alternatively, the Rockwool may be fixed at the front and rear of the trap leaving an air space in between.

The idea is that the bass will pass through to the Rockwool being partially absorbed at the same time while the upper mid and high frequencies will be scattered by the slats. An acoustically transparent fabric such as Hessian should be fitted over all Rockwool absorbers, not just for cosmetic reasons but also to keep the fibres out of the air. This kind of composite trap is shown in Figure 8.3.

In the likely event that you don't have enough room to mount a very deep bass absorber, it is possible to achieve significant absorption over much of the audio spectrum with a trap only 8" deep. One layer of 2" Rockwool slab is fixed directly to the wall while a second is fixed flush with the front of the trap as shown in Figure 8.4. A cosmetic fabric cover should be fitted, and if the trap is in an area where it is likely to to be knocked by people or equipment, expanded metal or wire mesh should be placed under the fabric to add a little strength. Once again, high frequency diffusers may be fitted in front of the trap if required.

Because of the limited depth of this trap, its low bass performance is restricted making it more suitable for use with near-field monitors than with large, full-range systems, but it does provide excellent absorption down to around 100Hz. The consensus seems to be that given the same amount of available space, a highly damped panel trap using roofing felt will give more bass absorption, though it will tend to reflect at mid and high frequencies.

TUNED TRAPS

If you know that you have problems at specific frequencies due to your room mode distribution, then lightly damped, tuned panel absorbers may be incorporated into the design to counter these. You can test for potential trouble spots by plugging a test oscillator into your monitor system and then sweeping through the 50Hz to 250Hz range to see if any obvious resonances show up. You can also identify dead spots in the same way. If you don't have access to a test oscillator, then you can set up a pure tone on a synth or sampler and then go through the lower octaves in semitone steps.

THE STUDIO

The traditional studio setup is to have a control room and a studio, the latter being the room where the musical performances take place. Changing recording practices have moved more of the actual recording process into the control room with MIDI keyboards, DI'd guitar and bass, and even vocals changing from one side of the glass to the other. But even so, a studio area is still necessary for recording loud, live instruments such as drums, piano or brass, and also for quieter instruments such as acoustic guitar.

Like the control room, the studio should be soundproofed to as high a degree as is practicable and the shell construction is essentially the same as for the control room should you decide to take that route. Also in common with control rooms is the ability of parallel walls to cause flutter echo problems, but these may be tamed by fixing just a few acoustic foam tiles to the offending walls - it's surprising how few you need to kill the flutter and you won't destroy the live effect of the room either.

VARIABLE ACOUSTICS

The main difference between the control room and the studio is that the internal treatment is less critical (unless for specialist applications such as voice-over work or classical recording) due to the intensive use of close miking techniques in pop and rock music recording. Nevertheless, there are those occasions on which a live environment combined with more ambient miking techniques is required, the obvious case being live drums.

The approach you take will depend on the space and budget you have available and separate, stone-lined live drum room are very nice if you can afford them. More often than not, a relatively untreated room can be pressed into surface as a drum room and the reverberation controlled by the use of movable screens or heavy drapes.

More common is the practice of building a single studio room that can be varied to cope with most eventualities. If the room is large enough, it is a fairly easy matter to arrange for one end to be quite absorbent, while the other end may have bare plaster walls and a solid wood or concrete floor. Instruments that require a live ambience can then be recorded at the live end while vocals can be recorded at the dead end. Double sided live/dead screens can be pressed into action enabling both types of environment to be used simultaneously should the session demand it.

Yet another possibility is to make the room completely live and then rely on drapes and movable screens to damp it down when a more controlled environment is required. The only real problem in working this way is that drapes and screens don't have any significant effect on the bass end of the spectrum so it may be as well to bass trap the room first. Even when the room is used in its live mode, having a well-controlled bass end gives a cleaner sound.

In a shell structure where plasterboard and studding are used to form the inner shell, the shell itself acts as a bass trap to some extent and so little additional trapping may be necessary. But in the case of solid brick or concrete walls, bass trapping will almost certainly be necessary. Well damped panel traps with light wooden or roofing felt panels will absorb the bass end while reflecting mid and high frequencies back into the room. Alternatively, you could opt for a full-range absorber based on a large depth of Rockwool and then cover the face of the trap with spaced wooden slats to disperse and reflect the high frequencies.

Figure 9.1 shows the floor plan of a multi-purpose room that might be practical for the larger home studio or the smaller commercial studio. One end of the room is deadened by drapes and a full width carpet, while the other end has movable drapes and a removable carpet allowing it to be either live or dead. As an alternative to drapes in the dead end of the room, you could use acoustic tiles, fabric covered Rockwool or even thick foam backed carpet spaced away from the wall on a 2x2" timber frame.

A couple of acoustic screens are recommended as they can be used reflective side out to kill flutter echoes by standing them at an angle to the walls or the dead side can be used to create a well-controlled vocal booth in one corner. The reflective side is also useful when recording drums or acoustic guitar to reflect sound back towards the microphones.

If space precludes this kind of room, a relatively untreated room will cope with most close miked requirements yet still be live enough for recording drums and guitar. Acoustic foam or fabric-covered Rockwool can be used to deaden about three feet either side of one corner making it possible to create a localised dead area for the recording of vocals. The corner may be boxed-in using a couple of acoustic screens if you need a particularly dead environment for voice-overs and suchlike. If you have no acoustic screens, these may be improvised by hanging blankets, towels or sleeping bags over drying frames or other improvised supports.

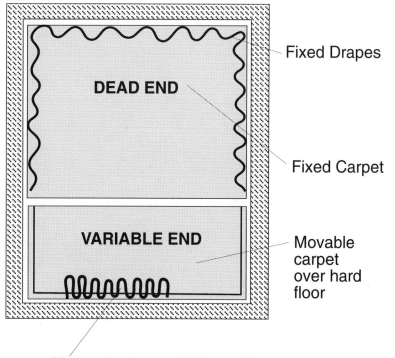

Figure 9.1: A General Purpose Room

MONITORS

The importance of a good monitoring system cannot be overestimated, yet all too often, an engineer will quite happily go ahead and mix a recording made using tens of thousands of pounds worth of recording equipment using a pair of domestic speakers costing around a couple of hundred pounds. No matter how good the recording equipment at your disposal, the only way you have of evaluating your work is via monitor loudspeakers so you really have to try to make the right decisions when it comes to choosing and setting up your monitor system. Furthermore, the type of monitor system you go for is significantly influenced by the type and size of control room available to you.

It is possible to mix on headphones, but this is not entirely satisfactory; first of all, stereo imaging effects sound different on headphones with the stereo sound stage often appearing to be inside the head of the listener, and maybe more importantly, the bass response of headphones varies tremendously, not only from model to model but also depending on how they fit the user. Nevertheless, headphones are a useful tool in listening for specific faults in a recording such as distortion, noise and clicks; loudspeakers are often more tolerant of these shortcomings.

THE IDEAL MONITOR

Most monitors take the form of a wooden box containing two or more loudspeakers; you connect them to a power amp and you're in business. But if the purpose of a loudspeaker is to sound as much as possible like the original sound, why are there so many types available and why do they all sound different?

Let's look at why most monitors contain more than one drive unit. The range of human hearing is very wide and a full-range studio monitor might be expected to cope with frequencies from as low as 30Hz up to in excess of 20kHz. Even smaller speakers are expected to cope with bass notes down to 50Hz or below - after all, the fundamental pitch of the lowest note on a bass guitar is around 42Hz and it would be useful to be able to hear that while mixing. In extreme cases, sounds such as organ pedal notes go down to 20Hz where they can be felt rather than heard. That's another area where headphones lose out, you can sometimes hear the low notes, but you can't really feel them!

CROSSOVERS

Unfortunately, there is no single design of loudspeaker drive unit that can cover the whole audio range with high enough fidelity and at a high enough level to be useful as a studio monitor. At a minimum, the sound has to be split into two frequency ranges and each range is handled by a particular type of speaker - the bass is handled by a woofer and the treble by a tweeter. Depending on the design, the crossover point between the

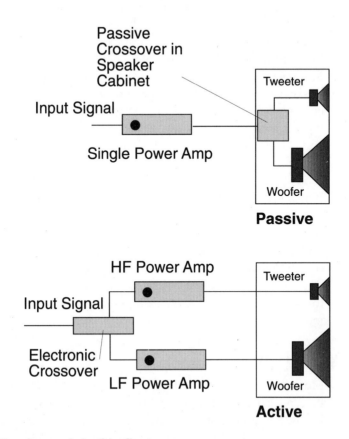

Figure 10.1: Passive and Active Systems

two speakers is usually in the 1.5kHz to 3kHz region, though it isn't an abrupt change - there is a progressive overlap.

In order to reproduce an accurate sound, the woofers and tweeters must be matched both electrically and acoustically and be driven from an electrical filter known as a crossover which directs the high frequencies to the tweeter and the low ones to the woofer. Most speakers use what is known as a passive crossover that filters the signal after it has left the power amplifier, but there are also active systems where a separate power amplifier is used to power each driver. Here an electronic crossover splits the signal before it reaches the amplifiers. These two approaches are outlined in Figure 10.1.

The passive crossover has the advantage that only one stereo power amplifier is needed to drive each speaker while an active one needs two stereo power amplifiers to drive one pair of two-way speakers. Active crossovers are more efficient than passive ones and may be designed to give more precise control over the crossover characteristics, but on the down side, they are more costly to implement.

MULTI-WAY

If a very deep bass response is necessary, then a larger woofer is normally employed, often in a correspondingly large cabinet, and the larger a loudspeaker drive unit, the less capable it is of handling higher frequencies. Consequently, we find that most large monitor systems include a separate mid-range speaker. Again, both active and passive versions are available.

To extend the available bass from smaller speaker enclosures, a technique known as porting is often employed. Taking into account the physical characteristics of the bass speaker, the volume of air in the box and the dimensions of the port, a design can be arrived at where the cabinet tuning adds a degree of lift to the bass end at the point where the woofer's natural response is falling off.

Careful tuning can result in very acceptable results, but attempts to overcompensate using this technique generally result in a boomy bass end that tends to favour a narrow range of notes. This may sound impressive for domestic playback, but is unacceptable for serious mixing as you don't know how much of the sound is on your recording and how much is being created by loudspeakers.

The other problem associated with a heavily tuned cabinet is that the bass response falls off quite rapidly below the frequency to which the port is tuned. By contrast, an unported design might not initially sound so impressive, but their more gentle bass roll-off characteristics often means that they are useful down to lower frequencies.

DRIVER TYPES

Though all loudspeakers might appear to be designed to achieve the same aims, different design philosophies are applied depending on whether the prime requisite is absolute loudness or tonal accuracy. Unfortunately, the technology does not yet exist to produce a monitor loudspeaker that will satisfy both requirements.

You may even wonder what are the differences between a studio monitor and a top-quality hi-fi speaker. Arguably, the aims are the same - to produce recorded music in the most realistic fashion possible. But because of the high sound levels at which studio monitors are often required to work, they have to be built to a far more rugged specification than domestic loudspeakers. They are also likely to be subjected to extremes of both high and low frequency from both miked acoustic and electronic instruments - and for long periods of time.

Domestic designs would soon overheat and sustain damage under these conditions, but a trend has emerged over the past few years to use a secondary monitoring system based around hi-fi speakers in order to evaluate the suitability of a mix for playback on a typical domestic system. These have to be used at correspondingly lower levels, but by switching back and forth between the main monitors and the secondary system, it is possible to produce a musical mix that 'travels well' - in other words, it should sound OK on a variety of domestic systems.

Some care needs to be exercised in selecting secondary monitors because many hi-fi speakers are deliberately voiced to sound impressive rather than being designed for greatest accuracy. This usually takes the form of added punch at the bass end and a little extra bite at the top end which can adversely affect your mixing decisions by giving a false impression of what is actually recorded onto tape.

WOOFERS

Woofers are usually conventional cone drivers, and the cone material may either be doped paper or a synthetic plastic material. Both types have their pros and cons, but purists often believe the paper types to be more accurate due to the better internal damping of paper-based cone materials. Synthetic cones often give a 'plumper' sound because they have a greater tendency to resonate. However, it would be wrong to base your choice of monitors purely on the materials employed - a proper listening test is the only way to make a valid judgment.

MID RANGE

Mid-range drivers tend to be either cone types or domes. The most accurate use soft domes made from doped fabric, though the trade-off is that these aren't so loud as some of the less accurate alternatives. Soft domes also have good dispersion characteristics which means they can produce an accurate sound not only directly in front of the cabinet, but also for listeners who may be standing to one side. This business of off-axis response is more important than it might initially seem and I'll be returning to it shortly.

TWEETERS

Tweeters are available in a multiplicity of forms, each with their pros and cons. As with mid-range drivers, soft dome tweeters are very accurate and free from significant resonances, but once again, they aren't the loudest tweeters available. Other designs make use of plastic or metal diaphragms and though these can generally produce higher sound pressure levels, they invariably suffer from resonances to a greater degree than soft-domed designs making them less accurate and more fatiguing to listen to over long periods.

Most efficient are the horn-loaded tweeters where a small pressure driver is connected to the end of a flared throat. The flare of the horn effectively matches the driver to the air in the room far more efficiently than any of the direct radiating tweeters resulting in a far higher available sound pressure level. But the down side is that reflections within the horn flare give rise to tonal colourations which lend horns a distinctive and rather aggressive sound. Currently, work is in progress aimed at designing an improved horn system where these artifacts are less obtrusive, but at the moment, horns are used mainly in systems where the ability to generate a very high sound level is more important than absolute fidelity.

DUAL CONCENTRIC

The dual-concentric system pioneered by Tannoy is a two-way system which makes use of a horn-loaded tweeter located in the exact centre of a cone mid/bass driver. The tweeter's horn is relatively small because the bass driver's cone acts as a physical extension to the flare, but because of this geometry, it isn't practical to implement a three-way design.

By far the greatest advantage of the dual concentric is its ability to present a point source of sound, regardless of how close the listener is to the speaker. On the other hand, the fact that the design is limited to two-way operation and the use of a horn-loaded tweeter gives the speakers a characteristic sound which, on some models is a little weak in the mid range.

Newer models have been developed by Tannoy which are considerably improved over their predecessors, but there is still a distinctive sound which engineers tend to either love or hate.

PHASE

Loudspeakers should not only have a nominally flat frequency response, they should also, as far as is possible, preserve the phase of all the individual harmonics that go to make up a sound. Sadly, this is easier said than done. With the exception of dual concentric designs, which present a point source of sound, the fact that two or three different drivers are covering the audio range means that the sound is coming from three different points in space.

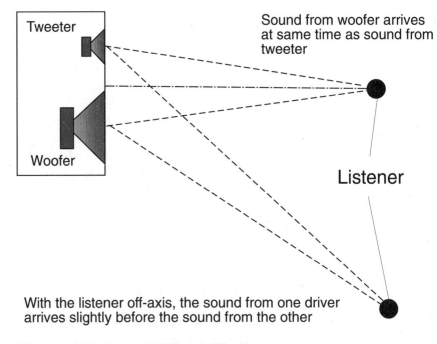

Figure 10.2: On and Off-axis Timing

If the listener is sitting directly in front of the monitor, then the sound from all three speakers will arrive at the same time, but if the listener is positioned either high or low with respect to the axis of the monitor, then the path lengths will be different. This in turn disturbs the phase relationship between the harmonics making up a sound. Figure 10.2 shows how this occurs in practice.

For this reason, it is normal for the drive units to be arranged one above the other rather than side by side. This means that once the speaker height is correct relative to the listener, the listener can then move freely from side to side without introducing phase problems. You will appreciate from this description that those engineers who lay monitors on their side in order to maintain a lower profile are also restricting their listening position to a narrower angle than if the monitors were mounted upright.

But there are other causes of phase error inherent in the design of the drivers themselves and the subject is too complex to go into here. Suffice it to say that phase response is just one of the factors that makes monitors sound different from each other when their published frequency responses indicates they ought to sound much the same.

OFF-AXIS RESPONSE

Just because a loudspeaker system produces a nominally flat frequency response when you are sitting directly in front of it doesn't mean that it will sound the same when you move a couple of feet to the left or right. That's because loudspeaker drive units don't project sound equally well in all directions - the response is optimised for listeners positioned on the axis of the speaker, but a significant amount of the sound is produced off the main axis. If this were not so, the level would drop dramatically as soon as you moved out of the direct line of fire of the speaker - and in any event, it couldn't really be prevented, even if this were desirable.

Sadly, the off-axis sounds invariably have a less flat frequency response than the on-axis sounds - high frequencies tend to be concentrated in a relatively narrow beam while very low bass projects just as well behind the speaker cabinet as it does in front. This usually results in the off axis sound being less bright than the on-axis sound.

Woofers, mid-range drivers and tweeters all have their own off-axis idiosyncrasies, but why is this important if the monitors are aimed directly at the listener. It's back to reverberation again - in a typical room, the listener hears the direct sound from the monitors plus the reverberant soundfield caused by sound reflecting from the walls and other surfaces.

Much of this reverberant soundfield is generated from the off-axis output of the monitors, so if the off-axis sound has a noticeably different frequency response to the direct sound, then the reverberant field will be coloured by this response. This is yet another reason why similarly specified loudspeakers can sound so different in the same listening room.

DIPS AND BUMPS

And finally, what appears to be a flat frequency response is almost certainly no such thing. Averaging techniques are used to make speaker responses look acceptable, but if you were able to see every tiny peak and dip in the response, you'd find narrow (and not so narrow) spikes and dips everywhere. The human ear is fairly tolerant of this kind of fine detail, but even so, this is yet another contributing factor to all monitors sounding different.

MONITOR SYSTEMS

Loudspeakers employing active crossover systems may have the amplifiers built into the speaker cabinets, or they may come as external rack-mount units along with a separate active crossover. The fully integrated type is the easiest to install because there is less wiring and no uncertainty as regards the choice of amplifier. If external amplifiers must be bought separately, consult the manufacturer's details with regard to power requirements and recommended brands.

Most small studios, especially home recording facilities, make use of passive loudspeakers so an appropriate stereo amplifier must be chosen. There used to be a widely held belief that if you chose an amplifier that was incapable of delivering the maximum power the speakers were designed to handle, the speakers would be safe from damage, but the reverse has transpired to be the case.

AMPLIFIER RATINGS

The current thinking is that if your speakers are rated to handle peaks of up to 100 Watts, then you should drive them with a 150 Watt amplifier. On the face of it, this makes little sense, but here is the underlying reasoning: Most modern loudspeakers are pretty tough, but if you overdrive them for long periods, the electrical current flowing through their voice coils generates more heat than can be dissipated.

This causes the temperature to build up until either the coil melts or the glue binding the coil to the former breaks down - either way, the result is disaster and you're in need of a re-cone job. It is also possible to damage a speaker by driving it so hard that the voice coil, in effect, bangs against the end-stops, but this sounds so horrible that only a fool would not turn the power down immediately. So you still don't see why you need an amp that's too big?

In normal music, the tweeter handles far less power than the bass unit because most of the energy of naturally produced music is at the bass end. This is also true of most electronically generated music, though the trend is to have more high frequency content than would occur in nature.

PEAKS

Music also has dynamics - there are peaks such as drum beats that are far louder than the average level, but these don't happen all the time; providing you don't drive the speakers against their end stops with these loud beats, and provided the signal is not distorted, damage is unlikely because these short bursts of energy aren't frequent enough to cause extreme voice coil heating.

But what happens if you try the same thing with an amplifier that is too small? Now the louder notes cause the amplifier to clip, and loud notes usually mean bass notes. These would normally not reach the tweeter because the crossover would filter them out, but once they are clipped, their new, squarer wave shape contains a huge amount of high frequency energy which is piped straight through the crossover to the tweeter. The result is a huge overload which heats the voice coil and fries it in no time flat.

PROTECTION

The situation is somewhat better with an active system because the clipping occurs after the crossover and so clipping at the bass end doesn't affect the clean signal being fed to the tweeter. Because of the somewhat cavalier attitude some engineers have towards their monitor systems, some manufacturers build in tweeter protection in the form of a low-voltage light built wired in series with the tweeter.

This relies on the fact that a bulb filament, when cold, has a low electrical resistance and so current can flow freely. But if the current is high enough to heat the filament, the resistance rises and the electrical energy is dissipated by the bulb, not by the tweeter. So, if you see flashing lights in the bass ports during a particularly heavy session, you aren't necessarily seeing things!

Both active and passive systems can also be protected by wiring electronic limiters before the power amplifiers to prevent clipping.

WIRING

Loudspeakers can pass quite heavy electrical currents so it is essential that the connecting cable has a low resistance. If lightweight cable is used, the cable resistance may be of the same order of magnitude as the speaker resistance (usually 8 ohms) which means that some of the energy is being dissipated by the cable as heat instead of reaching the monitors. Aside from losing level, the use of high resistance cable also reduces the intimate coupling between the amplifier and speaker which may result in the amplifier losing its ability to electrically damp the bass driver effectively. This can lead to a sloppy, uncontrolled bass sound.

There are specialist speaker cables around which can cost an absolute fortune, but many of these take things too far. Research has indicated that there is a subtle difference in sound caused by speaker cable resistance and capacitance, but beyond a certain limit, the difference is small enough to be considered insignificant. For amplifiers rated up to 150 Watts per channel or thereabouts, I'd be quite happy to use heavy-duty, twin-cored mains cable such as is sold for gardening appliances or conventional house wiring cable.

Keep the cables as short as possible and try to make the two lengths equal. Also, pay particular attention to the terminations at both the amplifier and loudspeaker ends to ensue that your cable is making the best possible connection.

If you are choosing an amplifier, either pick a reputable brand or a model that has been recommended to you by someone reliable, but above all, unless you're going for a really big system, pick an amplifier that doesn't need fan cooling - there are few more annoying things than noisy fans in the studio.

MONITORS AND ROOMS

From the previous chapters, it is evident that the sound of a monitor system is dependent not only on the monitors speakers themselves, but also on the type of room they are to be used in. A further consideration is the positioning of the speakers within the room as this too has a profound effect upon the final result. Then there's the question of what size monitors to use in a room of a given size, and whether they should be mounted on stands or recessed into wall soffits. I'll start out with a few generalisations that may make the choice easier.

If you are working in a small room such as a spare single bedroom or a cupboard under the stairs, then there's absolutely no point in trying to utilise a large, full-range loudspeaker system because the wavelength of the lowest notes the speakers can produce will be to long for the room to support. The result will be a confused and highly misleading bass end and a lot of unwanted bass rampaging through the rest of the building. Far better to pick a pair of loudspeakers that have a modest bass response, say down to 60Hz or so, and work with these - even in a larger room, a powerful bass end can often mask vital mid-range detail.

It's also safe to say that if you are working in a room that has little or no specific acoustic treatment, you'll get better results using a pair of small speakers fairly close to you than large ones at the opposite end of the room. This is because so-called near-field monitoring gives you a more favourable balance of direct and reflected sound so the room's own characteristics are less intrusive.

GEOMETRY

The ideal monitor geometry is to locate the speakers as two points on an equilateral triangle with the listening position being the third point. The speakers should be angled inwards so that the tweeters point directly at the listening position and the speaker height and angle should be adjusted so that the tweeters are directed towards the listening position in that plane also.

If more than one person is likely to be present at the mix, then the geometry may be changed slightly so that the speakers converge on a point a foot or so behind the engineer's head; this gives an acceptable stereo image for the greatest number of people. Figure 12.1 shows this arrangement.

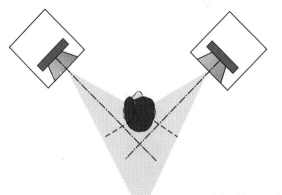

Acceptable listening area

Figure 12.1: Optimum Monitor Geometry

Where possible, the speakers should be positioned along the longest wall of the room and, unless they are specifically designed with soffit mounting in mind, they should be mounted on rigid, non-resonant stands a few inches clear of the wall. As stressed earlier, monitors work best when the drive units are aligned vertically rather than horizontally, but if you feel the need to put a pair of small speakers on your meter bridge lengthwise, you may find you get the best result with the tweeters innermost. That's because mounting them the other way generally results in too great a distance between the tweeters relative to the listener's distance from the speakers resulting in a stereo image with a noticeable hole in the middle.

STANDS

Open-frame, metal speaker stands are ideal for small and mid-sized monitors, though you can use chipboard boxes filled with sand as an alternative. As chipboard reflects sound, it is best to cover such stands with foam rubber or some equally effective sound absorber. Some perfectionists even fill their tubular steel stands with sand to increase the mass and reduce the resonance. There's also a school of thought that advocates standing the speakers on blobs of Blu Tak rather than directly onto the stands in order to decouple some of the cabinet vibrations.

When using larger monitors with an extended bass response, it is important that the cabinet vibration is not allowed to couple into the structure of the room; sound travels faster through solids than it does in air and it's possible that structurally borne sound could reach the listener before the direct sound from the loudspeakers which plays havoc with the stereo imaging. One approach to this is to decouple the speakers by resting them on sheets of foam neoprene.

CORNERS

It's very tempting to mount speakers in corners out of the way, but in practice, this is not a good idea. The reason is all to do with the fact that at very low frequencies, the sound radiates from the monitors omnidirectionally - in other words, you get as much bass coming out of the back and sides of the cabinet as you do from the front. If the room has

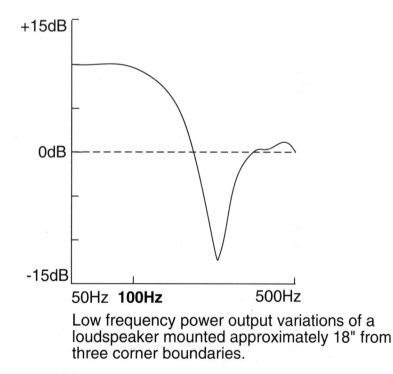

Low frequency power output variations of a loudspeaker mounted approximately 18" from three corner boundaries.

Figure 12.2: Effect of Corner Mounting on Frequency Response.

solid walls, this low frequency energy will bounce back into the room and combine with the direct sound - but as it is delayed by the time it takes to reach the wall and bounce back, it will be out of phase with the direct sound at some frequencies and in phase at others.

If a single wall is involved, the reflected low end gives a slight bass lift but nothing too serious - in fact, many speakers rely on it. If you now put the speaker into a corner where two walls are involved, there are two sets of reflections, both in-phase with each other, which will further interfere with the direct sound. This produces both humps and dips in the bass response, the precise frequencies of which depend on how close to the walls the monitor is actually positioned. If we now go one further and put the speakers in a corner and position them the same height from the floor as they are from the walls, we have the worst possible case where the humps and bumps in the bass response can be hugely misleading. Figure 12.2 shows how the frequency response of a monitor can be affected by mounting it in this way.

The conclusion that can be drawn from this scenario is that if monitors do have to be mounted close to the corners, they should be positioned so that the distances from the back wall, the side wall and the floor are as

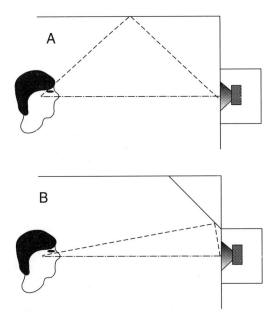

Note: By fitting a sloping surface close to the monitor, as in diagram B, the early reflection path is considerably shortened.

Figure 12.3: Sloping Soffit Surround

different as possible. In this way, the reflected sounds are not in-phase with each other and so will produce less serious perturbations in the bass response of the monitor.

If corner mounting is inevitable, at least make sure that the monitor-to-floor distance is radically different to the monitor-to-wall distance and pick a speaker with a modest bass response or one that rolls off smoothly. A marginal improvement can sometimes be effected by stuffing the space behind the speakers with Rockwool.

SOFFIT MOUNTING

Most large pro studios use Soffit mounted monitors, mainly to keep them out of the way. Because they are mounted in solid alcoves, all the bass energy is forced to radiate into the room over a 180° angle rather than being allowed to radiate over 360° so there will be twice as much bass entering the room than if the same speakers were mounted free standing. This is allowed for in the speaker design - ordinary monitor speakers mounted in recessed soffits will almost certainly appear to be disproportionally bass heavy.

Some designers recess their monitors into flat surfaces while others build in reflective surfaces that slope away from the monitors as shown in figure 12.3. The theory behind this latter approach is that it forces the early reflections to follow the original sound very closely. In this way, the early reflections contribute to the loudness of the sound without causing serious phase errors. As in most areas of studio design, there are those who go along with this theory and other who vigorously denounce it.

NEAR-FIELD MONITORING

If a studio is equipped with a decent pair of full-range monitors, you may wonder why the majority of engineers still do much of their work on a pair of hi-fi speakers perched on the meter bridge of the desk. There are several reasons, possibly the most valid being that it gives the engineer some idea of how the mix will sound on a home hi-fi system. Furthermore, because of the large disparities between control rooms and monitoring systems in different studios, visiting engineers may bring along a familiar pair of speakers to use as a reference, and by using these in the near field, the effect of the control room acoustic on the perceived sound is minimal. It is for this very same reason that many studios are equipped with Yamaha NS10 near-field speakers - it's not that they are particularly good, but there are so many around that they do, at least, represent some form of common standard.

It is not uncommon for engineers to take a cassette or DAT tape of a mix back home to check on their own hi-fi systems and a lot can be revealed about a mix by playing it back on a car cassette player or a ghetto blaster; if it sounds good under these conditions, it will almost certainly sound good on the radio.

MONITOR EQUALISATION

Not so many years ago, it was considered essential to incorporate a graphic equaliser in the monitor chain in order to tune out any bumps or dips in the frequency response caused by the acoustic of the room. The theory was that a measurement microphone with a very flat frequency response would be set up at the listening position and then a wide-band noise source fed through the monitors. A multi-band signal analyser would be connected to the microphone and the equaliser tweaked until the analyser proclaimed a flat response. It sounds too good to be true doesn't it? And it is!

The lumps and dips in the room response are caused by the room having different reverberation times at different frequencies, mainly due to the room mode distribution, and reverberation is an effect that is related to time. By equalising the feed to the monitor speakers, we may fool a microphone measuring a steady-state signal into believing that everything is OK, but equalisation affects frequency response, not time. In other words, we are trying to correct a time-domain problem using a frequency domain solution.

Sadly, because music isn't a steady-state signal, but a continually varying one, the cure doesn't work. What is more, because of the nature of psychoacoustics, the human ear pays most attention to the direct sound from the monitors and rather less attention to the reverberant field. If we don't equalise the monitors, we perceive a good monitoring system as producing a good sound in a bad room. If we then equalise the monitors, we hear the same bad room, but this time we are also hearing the wrong sound from the monitors - clearly a step in the wrong direction.

A room is, if you like, a mechanical equaliser, and if you want to equalise it, then you have to do that by mechanical means such as trapping. It may be permissible to add small amounts of equalisation to monitors to make the sound more to your liking, but trying to correct room problems this way leads to even bigger discrepancies between what you think you hear on the speakers and what you've actually recorded on tape.

BUDGET ROOMS

You can learn a lot from professional studio design, and you don't have to be building a professional studio to put it to good use. Even if you are doing all your recording and mixing in a single small room somewhere in your house, you can improve the result by paying a little attention to the monitoring and the acoustics.

Take the example of a bedroom studio - the acoustics aren't likely to be any worse than a typical lounge and the presence of a bed is good news in acoustic terms as it traps a fair amount of mid and high frequency sound. If the bedroom/studio is upstairs and has a wooden floor, this will trap out some of the bass as will lightweight internal doors and wardrobes and suchlike.

MONITORS

In such an environment a near-field monitor setup is to be recommended because it will be less affected by the room acoustics and it will also make it possible to monitor at quieter levels while still getting enough level at the listening position. An arrangement with the speakers placed around three feet in front of the engineers chair and about four feet apart should do fine.

Try to set the speakers up vertically rather than laying them on their sides and try to mount them on something solid rather than just propping them up with whatever comes to hand.

MIXER

The ideal place for the mixer is in the middle of the room, but this is seldom practical so it usually ends up facing the wall. This isn't so bad in a small room, but avoid the other situation where you are sitting with your back close to a wall. The reason for this warning is that sound reflects back from walls, and when you are within a few inches of a wall, a very noticeable rise in bass is evident. This is less apparent with lightweight partition walls, but sitting with your back up against a brick wall will give you a totally unreal perception of the bass end.

Try to arrange your mixer and monitors so that they are positioned as symmetrically as possible in the room and ensure that the speakers aren't obscured by equipment, furniture or rubber plants! You should have an uninterrupted view of both speakers from your normal mixing position.

IMPROMPTU ACOUSTICS

If you can set up your keyboard system along the wall behind you, it will help to break up any reflected sound as will any shelves or other irregularly shaped furniture. In the event that the room is very narrow and reflections from the side walls are causing trouble, improvise by hanging a quilt or blanket on each side wall directly adjacent to your mixing position.

Another point to keep in mind is that no matter how good or bad your room sounds, after a while your ears will become fatigued and making meaningful decisions will become difficult. At times like these, and directly before starting a mix, I suggest you play some of your favourite records or CDs through the monitor system to give you some kind of reference to aim for. The ears are very forgiving of sound systems, but they do like to have a reference point!

LARGER HOME STUDIOS

If you can dedicate a whole room to your control room but don't want to do too much in the way of acoustic treatment, then I'd suggest that you stick with near-field monitoring and hang an absorbing fabric-covered Rockwool panel, about three feet along each side, on the side walls directly adjacent to your listening position. This will kill any flutter echo. If the room is still too live, a similar absorber may be hung over the mixing console around 12" from the ceiling using screw-in hooks and plug chain.

The floor should be fully carpeted and heavy curtains over the windows will help too. Try to include some soft furnishings, even if it's just a sofa at the back of the room, and follow the rules on monitor location, keeping away from corners and siting along the longer wall if practical to do so. To evaluate your room, there are few better tests than playing some well-known recordings through the system with no equalisation. If you like the sound you're getting, then you can work with it.

If you have to record and perform in the same room, then try to fix up a dead corner as far away from the tape machine as possible in which to do vocals. The clicks and whirrs of tape machines have an annoying habit of ending up on tape, especially when you're doing drop-ins.

TOTAL TREATMENT

Should you want to make your control room suitable for more serious mixing, then there are several approaches you can take, but unless you have the facility to measure the room's performance, it is best to use as little treatment as you can get away with. If you're starting with a bare

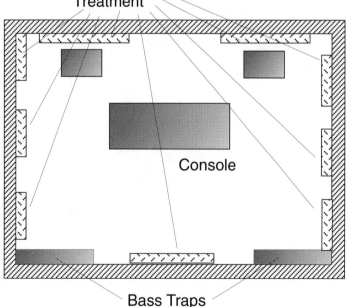

Distributed Absorbent Surface Treatment

Console

Bass Traps

The room shown has parallel walls as that is the situtuation normally encountered when setting up a budget studio.

Figure 13.1: Distributed Absorption

room, a fitted carpet is a good start as it dries up some of the mid and high frequency reverberation straight away. If the room is a lightweight shell or has an inner plasterboard-on-battens wall, then you may be lucky and need no further bass trapping; a little distributed mid/high absorber on the side and front walls combined with the obligatory sofa at the rear may be all you need.

WHAT SYSTEM?

At this point you should decide whether you want to lean towards the LEDE philosophy or go for a room which is uniformly absorbent all over. A living room is more or less equally absorbent throughout, so if you like the sound of your stereo system in the lounge, the chances are you'll be happy working in a similarly treated control room. Using 2" Rockwool in fabric covered frames, you could fit panels extending from around two feet from the floor to around two feet from the ceiling and space these by a further two feet as shown in Figure 13.1. If a panel on one wall faces bare wall on the other side, then flutter echoes will be avoided, even in a room with parallel sides which, after all, is what most of us have to work with.

If the walls are solid, then a couple of well-damped, limp-membrane (roofing felt) panel traps in the back corners would probably be a good

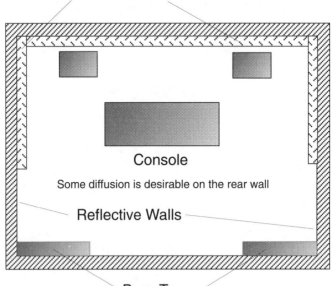

Absorbent Surface Treatment

Console

Some diffusion is desirable on the rear wall

Reflective Walls

Bass Traps

The room shown has parallel walls as that is the situtuation normally encountered when setting up a budget studio.

Figure 13.2: Absorption at Monitor End

move. These would, typically, start from the corners and cover about a quarter of the rear wall area each. Of course, without proper measurement, this can only be an approximate guide so try to be flexible in your approach. For example, the absorptive mid/high panels could be made to hang from hooks on the wall allowing you to fit a few at a time while conducting listening tests using known CDs and your intended monitoring system. If the room is too reverberant, the stereo imaging and overall sound will be a little fuzzy, but if too much mid/high damping is applied, then you may well find you're left with a bass boom. The happy medium should be fairly evident. If you have enough ceiling height, then mid/high or limp membrane bass traps may be fixed to or suspended from the ceiling.

In smaller rooms, it is impossible to adequately diffuse rear-wall reflections so many designers prefer to 'remove' the rear wall entirely as far as acoustic considerations are concerned. This is achieved by making the whole of the rear wall into a wide-range trap and the best budget solution may well be the roofing-felt type, limp membrane trap covered with pleated fabric to absorb the upper mid and high frequencies.

LEDE

Should you prefer the LEDE option, then similar techniques may be employed except the absorbent panels should be concentrated in the front half of the room and an area of absorber should be fixed to the ceiling or suspended over the mixing console. If the monitors are to be mounted in soffits, then the cavity space around them can be usefully employed by building in bass trapping. This treatment falls far short of a full LEDE treatment, but providing you use sensible monitors that don't produce more bass than the room can handle, you should be able to achieve very good results. Figure 13.2 shows how you might arrange such a room.

SUMMARY

Having read the previous chapters, you should now be in a better position to understand the problems you may encounter in setting up your studio and how to tackle them. Soundproofing is usually high on the agenda, especially for studios working in residential areas, and while a complete cure may not be practical because of space or budget constraints, you'll almost certainly be able to make a significant improvement without going to great expense.

SOURCE

Because sound isolation rarely approaches perfection, you may be able to meet the problem half way by generating less noise in the first place. Near-field monitoring offers a double bonus to the small studio owner because it means the overall monitor level can be less loud than with a system located further away from the listener, and the effect of the room acoustic is minimised. It is also possible to monitor using headphones for recording and overdubbing, only turning to the monitors when mixing.

Sound generating equipment will cause less of a problem if it is isolated from the floor of a room, especially if the floor is made of wood; one studio owner replaced his traditional drum kit with a set of electronic pads only to find that the physical thump of the bass drum pedal still sounded loud and clear in the room below. A little improvisation can save a great deal of expense and mounting instrument amplifiers on rubber foam or even inflated inner tubes can cut down structurally-borne sound quite significantly.

DI'ING

Rock guitars may now be DI'd in a quite satisfactory manner using so-called speaker simulators. These plug into the speaker outlet of an instrument amplifier and filter the sound in such a way as to imitate the colouration of the speaker. The output is a low-level signal which can be DI'd directly into a mixing console, and one of the great advantages of this approach, apart from the lack of noise, is that what you hear over the monitors is exactly the sound going to tape. If the guitarist sits close to the studio monitors, even feedback effects can be achieved!

OPTIMUM ACOUSTICS

While soundproofing follows fairly predictable physical rules, acoustic treatment is less easily pinned down. Though there are well documented physical laws governing the way sound is absorbed and reflected, the difficulties in measuring the results and the unpredictable variables involved make acoustic design as much an art as a science. Even then, a control room designed to give a specific performance will behave differently when it contains half a dozen extra people and a stack of MIDI keyboards.

But more important is the fact that there is so much much disagreement as to what constitutes the ideal monitoring environment. At the end of the day, we have to keep firmly in mind the the end result of our efforts, the record, CD or cassette, is going to be listened to over small or medium powered speakers in a variety of imperfect domestic rooms or in cars - not in some over-designed control room with monitors the size of tumble-dryers.

MONITOR REQUIREMENTS

It is important to listen to commercial mixes over full-range speakers because that's the only way to tell what is going on right at the bottom of the audio spectrum; a pair of small domestic monitors may well miss out the lowest octave completely. Nevertheless, unless the control room is adequately large and properly designed to handle such monitors, the results are likely to be more misleading than simply relying on small speakers all along.

Even when a mix is checked on a full-range monitor system, it is still wise to double check that it sounds good on a typical domestic two-way speaker - hence the tendency to use compact, two-way devices as near-field monitors. Another advantage of near-field monitoring is that the weaker bass end leaves the vulnerable mid-range more exposed so errors or distortions are more likely to show up.

In any event, it cannot be stressed too highly that whatever the room and whatever the monitor system installed in it, your ears need a reference, and listening to some known material over the system before the session starts (and again before mixing) is so much safer than 'flying blind'. Even in your own studio where you may think you know the sound well, your perception will change depending on the length of time you've been working, the level at which you've been monitoring, and other factors. For example, adding treble or processing the sound with an exciter will tend to make you less sensitive to the actual amount of top end in the mix, and when you compare it side by side with a commercial recording, you may find you've gone well over the top without even noticing it.

REALISTIC AIMS

Commercial control rooms are designed to criteria simply not achievable in the smaller studio or home facility. They have inner shells designed with non-parallel walls, specially shaped ceilings and carefully calculated trapping. Corners are avoided and the geometry is carefully planned. For those of us setting up a budget home studio or a small-scale commercial facility, many of these aims simply cannot be realised. We usually have to make do with a rectangular room of less than optimum proportions, but then that isn't so bad because that's exactly the description of a typical living room and most of those can sound OK with the right speaker system installed.

In may ways, it's what we do to convert our typical living room into a studio that upsets the sound. Out goes the furniture which is normally distributed in a sufficiently random manner to offer some diffusion and in come racks of flat fronted, highly reflective equipment. Out go the absorbent items such as three-piece suites and curtains, and instead we have bare control room windows and flat-topped mixing consoles.

RATIONAL APPROACH

But with a little thought based on the information presented so far, many of these undesirable effects can be minimised. Fitting a carpet to the floor will take a lot of ring out of the room and a nice soft sofa at the back for the clients will do wonders. The overall liveness can be cut down by hanging patches of heavy drape a few inches from the wall but don't go too mad, we don't want to be left with a booming bottom end with no high frequency reverberation to balance it out. The absolute worst thing you can do is to carpet all the surfaces in the room because then you soak up all the upper mid and top leaving a room that is boxy and muddy, dominated by the untrapped bass and lower mid.

Try making the surface area of your absorbers around four square yards to compensate for a missing three-piece suite and you won't go too far wrong. Bass trapping probably isn't vital so long as you pick a pair of speakers with a smooth bass roll-off. Wooden floors and plasterboard lined rooms also have the natural ability to trap out some of the bass. A non-ported monitor design that rolls off gradually below 80Hz or so will work far better in an untrapped room than a ported model that props up the bass down to 50Hz or so and then cuts off rapidly.

And finally, remember that the most important piece of equipment in your studio is your own hearing. You can make good mixes on the most rudimentary equipment so long as you remain aware of its limitations and keep comparing it to a known reference recording played over the same equipment. Try to avoid the temptation to monitor at loud levels for long periods as this not only clouds the judgment and changes the perceived musical balance, it can also cause permanent hearing damage. As a general rule, monitor your mix at the kind of level you expect it to be played at by the end listener, and restrict loud listening to short periods.

AIR CONDITIONING

Full studio air conditioning systems are beyond the scope of this book; they involve large and complicated ducting systems complete with acoustic baffles and isolation mounts for the pumping machinery. Many professional systems cost in excess of the entire budget for a medium sized commercial studio. Having said that, most studios require more in the way of air cooling than an actual change of air; the biggest problem is heat generated by equipment and lighting, not clients using up all the oxygen. In such cases, a heat exchanger air-cooling system may be quite adequate so long as the doors are opened once in a while to change the air.

These come in two types: the through-the-wall unit and the split system. Both work on the same principle whereby a fan recycles the room air over a cooled element while the heat is dissipated outdoors by means of a fan-cooled radiator. The inner and outer units are connected by pipework, but with the through-the-wall system, the whole unit is built into one box which must be mounted half in and half out of the room via a large hole in the wall. Because these devices are not designed with sound isolation in mind, the barrier between the inside and the outside of the building is usually a thin piece of sheet steel with a little foam stuck to it - no real deterrent to loud noises.

A through-the-wall system can be quietened by fitting an external cowl lined with foam or Rockwool, but it needs to be large enough to allow the air to pass through unrestricted. A far more efficient method of cooling is to employ a split system where the inner and outer elements are physically separate and are joined only by narrow-bore pipes. A further advantage of the split system is that one external unit can feed more than one internal unit so you could cool both your studio and control room.

The actual power of the system depends on the size of room it is to cool and the amount of heat normally generated in the room which you can calculate by adding up the power requirements of all your bits of gear. And don't forget to add on the power of all the lighting. Whoever supplies your system will be able to calculate the power you need so long as you have these figures to hand.

Unlike the large air-conditioning systems that use large ducts and very low air velocities in order to keep the noise down, the air is blown from a typical cooler at a fairly brisk rate and the noise generated is comparable with that produced by a fan heater. For this reason, coolers are often turned off during takes. The outside unit can also create quite a lot of fan noise and you should check the specifications of your intended purchase to make sure the fan doesn't annoy the neighbours more than your studio does. To find a supplier, check out Air Conditioning in Yellow Pages.

MATERIALS

Most of the materials used in sound isolation and acoustic treatment can be bought from builders' suppliers, notably Rockwool, fibre-glass, plasterboard, flooring chipboard, roofing felt, insulation-board and timber. Items such as barrier mat, half-round door gasket, compression latches, specially perforated peg-board, Lamella flooring, neoprene machine mounts and so forth can only be obtained from a specialist supplier of acoustic materials. One of the largest suppliers in the UK is: Siderise Ltd., Southsea Road, Kingston-Upon-Thames, England. Tel: 081-549 6389 or Fax:: 081-546 2246. This company can also offer advice on installations using their materials. Other specialist companies may be located via Yellow Pages.

Available Now:

The Creative Recording Series

Written by Paul White, the CREATIVE RECORDING series is rapidly being accepted as the standard work for home recordists and studio technicians alike, and indeed has become required reading on some academic courses.

Volume One:
EFFECTS and PROCESSORS

The first book in the CREATIVE RECORDING series has been hailed as the "ultimate studio accessory" and David Ward, founder of the highly respected Gateway School of Recording wrote *"This is the book I wish I'd written myself"*.

The pressure on both studios and home recordists to keep up with the very latest in technology can mean that budgets get stretched to the limit, despite the rapidly falling cost of high-quality equipment.

When each new acquisition seems to expose as many problems in your recording system as it solves, it becomes increasingly necessary to choose equipment which is precisely suited to your needs and then for you to get the very best out of it on a day to day basis.

Of course, the instruction manual is always there to show you exactly how a piece of equipment works. What it seldom does is explain *when* it is needed, *why* it is necessary and *where* it should be used...

Building to a complete series, CREATIVE RECORDING has been written to provide all those with an active involvement in sound recording with a comprehensive overview of modern recording practice.

Volume One: EFFECTS and PROCESSORS is a modern sourcebook of information on all the different types of effects and processors currently found in the studio.

Chapters cover Compressors & Limiters, Reverberation, Gates and Expanders, Delay, Pitch Shifters, Patchbays, Enhancers, Equalisers and Panners as well as related areas such as Mixing, Production, and MIDI techniques. This book provides the most comprehensive coverage of this aspect of the recording process to date.

CREATIVE RECORDING Volume One: EFFECTS and PROCESSORS by Paul White ISBN 1 870951 04 2 £9.95

Volume Two:
MICROPHONES and
RECORDING TECHNIQUES

This, the second volume in the CREATIVE RECORDING series, takes the mystery out of choosing and using microphones in a recording environment The microphone is the first step in the recording chain, and mistakes made here are impossible to remedy later. MICROPHONES and RECORDING TECHNIQUES is designed to help you avoid making these mistakes.

Volume One was concisely written in plain English in order to convey the maximum information in the minimum time. Volume Two takes exactly the same approach and starts out by explaining how studio microphones work, what are the strengths and weaknesses of the different types available and, most importantly, how to choose the right one for the job in hand.

It then goes on to cover specific techniques for vocal and speech recording, classical stereo recording and various methods of miking both rock and classical instruments - from the drum kit to the grand piano! DI techniques for guitars and basses are also discusses along with their pros and cons, and there's a section dedicated entirely to PZM mics. Extensive use of illustrations and photographs make even the more advanced aspects clear and easy to understand.

CREATIVE RECORDING Volume Two: MICROPHONES and RECORDING TECHNIQUES by Paul White ISBN 1 870951 07 7 £9.95